HOW TO BE A
BAD BOTANIST

HOW TO BE A
BAD BOTANIST

SIMON BARNES

Illustrations by Cindy Lee Wright

**SIMON &
SCHUSTER**

London · New York · Sydney · Toronto · New Delhi

First published in Great Britain by Simon & Schuster UK Ltd, 2024

Page 188: Illustration adapted from Sphenopteris, vintage
engraving © Patrick Guenette, Dreamstime.com
Page 220: Reference image © Beth Chatto's Plants & Gardens

1 3 5 7 9 10 8 6 4 2

Simon & Schuster UK Ltd
1st Floor
222 Gray's Inn Road
London WC1X 8HB

Simon & Schuster: Celebrating 100 Years of Publishing in 2024

www.simonandschuster.co.uk
www.simonandschuster.com.au
www.simonandschuster.co.in

Simon & Schuster Australia, Sydney
Simon & Schuster India, New Delhi

A CIP catalogue record for this book
is available from the British Library

Hardback ISBN: 978-1-3985-1891-9
eBook ISBN: 978-1-3985-1892-6

Typeset in Palatino by M Rules
Printed and Bound in the UK using 100% Renewable Electricity
at CPI Group (UK) Ltd

MIX
Paper | Supporting
responsible forestry
FSC
www.fsc.org
FSC® C171272

This one's for the hyacinth girl

CONTENTS

Not knowing the name of the tree,
I stood in the flood
of its sweet scent.

Matsuo Bashō

Without the name any flower is more or less
a stranger.

John Burroughs

Yellow horned poppy

1

THE BOMBSHELL

Before enlightenment chop wood, carry water. After
enlightenment chop wood, carry water.

Zen saying

My enlightenment came with an atom bomb. Not like – with.
As a student of Zen finds enlightenment in a hand-clap, so
I reached a new understanding of life, its meaning and its
possibilities after an encounter with a bomb. I went to look
for birds, but I was forced to confront the deaths of 146,000
people. As a result, I left with an appreciation of life I hadn't
known before. I am now a bad botanist: and if that seems a
trivial mental adjustment after contemplating death on such
a scale, I will attempt in the course of these pages to point
out, in the gentlest possible manner, that this would be an
error of judgement.

I was on Orford Ness, one of the strangest places in Britain.
I was researching a project about the Rothschild List, which

was one of the great pioneering events in the history of nature conservation. Charles Rothschild, wealthy, keenly aware of his duties as a public man and absolutely mad for nature, compiled with friends and colleagues a list of 284 wild places 'worthy of preservation'. From this came the network of county wildlife trusts that exists across Britain. One of these sites was Orford Ness.

This list was published in 1916, at a time when British people and their government had other things on their minds than nature. In the midst of war, nature seems trivial: a luxury none of us can afford. That, too, is an error of judgement, but by the time the list was published, Orford Ness was being used for warlike purposes. Aeroplanes had only been around for a dozen years; on the Ness they were developed as weapons of war.

Orford Ness is a spit of shingle 10 miles long off the coast of Suffolk; it is attached to the mainland by a strip 100 yards across. It is at once both accessible and cut-off: easy to get to but equally easy to isolate. For some people it's a great place to look for birds, for others it's a great place for bombs: it's all in the way these things take you. When the First World War was over it was used for military research in bombs and ballistics: here you can fire a bullet a very long way without very much to get in the way, certainly not people. The place was used for testing bombs during the Second World War, and then in the Cold War it was used for the development of over-the-horizon radar. It was also used for testing still more deadly weapons and was designated an Atomic Weapons Research Establishment. Its military past is part of its enthralling and deeply uncomfortable present.

You get there by boat: there's a National Trust ferry from

the pleasant little Suffolk town of Orford, available on certain days of the year. Once there, you walk. It's a hostile place, in two senses: it's very low and very flat; on most of it you are the highest thing for a mile or more, exposed to the weather in a way that's subtly and cumulatively disturbing. The near century – the place came to the Trust in 1993 – of warlike use has naturally left its mark; there are many military buildings of uncompromising functionality. They seem curiously cheap after all those years of weather: ugly and uncomfortable huts clustered round the landing stage, and, dominating the southern end, three strange buildings: great concrete lids balanced on concrete pillars like a modernist homage to Stonehenge.

They are unexpectedly named pagodas and it's here that the casing of atom bombs was tested. No nuclear explosions were scheduled for Orford Ness: the people working there had the job of making sure that the real things didn't explode in transit over some friendly or unfriendly nation. They also tested ballistics, including rockets: jets flew over the Ness firing rockets from 50 feet into a spot called King's Marsh. I had been inside the pagodas on a previous trip, rotting and abandoned places full of messages about the sinister futilities of war. Last century's wars were abandoned here, but as we all know, proper up-to-date versions are being avidly worked on elsewhere. This is history, and pretty awful history at that. History that tells you warfare is as ancient and as modern as the new day's sun over the sea.

And in one of those huts there's an atom bomb. It's about 11 feet long and if you hugged it, your fingertips would meet. One observer noted that you could put it in the back of a Volvo estate if you put the seats down. It's disarmed, of course, but there it is, in all its frank simplicity: a WE177, serial number QV0679, colour white, natty fins so it falls straight when you drop it from the air – about the size of the bomb that was dropped on Hiroshima in 1945.

I visited Hiroshima. I went by train. I waited on the platform until the sign whirled and clicked round to read:

Hiroshima

To most of us Hiroshima is an event, not a living city with people going to school and doing the shopping and coming home from work. I was about to catch a train to the place where 146,000 people were killed by a small Volvo-portable bomb. I went there and I wept, as everyone who goes there must, and then a few years later, as I walked the shingle pathways of Orford Ness, I remembered my tears. I also remembered Sadako Sasaki, dying from leukaemia aged twelve. She made origami cranes, knowing that if you make a thousand of them, a real crane will grant you a wish. The leukaemia was a side-wipe of the bomb: the origami crane is now a symbol of it.

I walked on across Orford Ness, looking for birds as I always do. I found not a crane but a great white egret, tall, slender and elegant, a very acceptable stand-in. Notices warned me: 'Unexploded ordnance – please keep to the visitor route'. Trespassers would be blown up? I kept. A hare, scampering away from me in an unbothered sort of way, ignored the notices but cantered on, unexploded.

After a while I decided to sit. The idea was for a bit of a seawatch. Seawatching has all the intellectual stimulation of staring at a fire: the thinking person's television. You tell yourself you're looking for harbour porpoises and gannets and scoters, but mostly you're looking at waves and sky while your mind goes wherever it chooses. It's a pleasant activity: soothing, not-un-Zenish, with its no-mind possibilities. The North Sea was brown with sediment and lumpy, a little fizz of Guinness-froth at the top of the modest waves.

The shingle was pretty chunky: you could hold maybe a dozen stones in a single hand. Orford Ness is all shingle: it has been gathered there across the centuries by the process of longshore drift. It wasn't the best shingle for sitting on: I could feel, it seemed, each individual stone through the seat of my trousers. But it was OK. I sat knees-up, elbows on knees, binoculars to my eyes: a good steady base for prolonged staring. All birders know how to sit that way; it's also the perfect position for not seeing marine mammals. Like a Zen master, my sitting was devoid of porpoise.

I know, of course, that I was fooling myself. I knew I was seeking not seabirds and sea mammals but some kind of accommodation with that white cylinder in the hut – that conveniently sized thing that could kill 146,000 people. I raised the glasses and stared at the porpoiseless waves. I lowered them and stared at the shingle all around me. I was quite tiny beneath the East Anglian sky.

After a while I was aware that there were plants on either side of me: plants growing out of the shingle. Which is impossible. Obviously you can't grow plants on a heap of stones. Except that there they were. Growing. What's more some of them had flowers: huge yellow flowers 3 inches across, bright and beautiful as you could wish. The plants had thick leaves; some of them looked like school-dinner cabbage. They grew in little clumps, here and there in this high-point of the shingle, a good few steps beyond the tide-line, mostly knee-high, some of the clumps a bit bigger.

What a ridiculous place to be a plant. There seemed to be nothing whatsoever in this place to make plant life possible, still less agreeable. Why not choose rainforest or a nice back garden in Pinner or the Entangled Bank that Darwin wrote about? There was no end to the number of things wrong with this place if you happened to be a plant. There was no earth. Pebbles are always in motion, so there's no stability. A pebble bed is full of spaces, so it can't hold any water. There's nowhere among the pebbles for storing nutrients. And the whole place was full of salt: you could taste it in the air, it coated every pebble, it was as much a part of the place as the sky and the waves. Take a trowel and dig in just about any normal plant here and it would curl up and die in a matter of hours.

Yet here on Orford Ness – on the beach of death, a place whose business had been the development of efficient ways of killing people, a task at which we had been getting better and better for nearly a hundred years – was a ragged and rugged community of plants making a living in a place where no life should be. This stretch of shingle was a place of hope, not despair, and, as is appropriate for all thoughts of war, there was a poppy.

Notes and photographs taken on the spot and added to later research revealed that there were three species of plants beside me: sea pea, sea kale and the glorious yellow horned poppy. The poppies were in flower: the horns would come later, long seed cases up to a foot long. The leaves had a leathery look and feel to them, as if they'd been made by some inventive person with a needle. They were coated in wax, the better to retain water. I didn't know it then, but each plant had a taproot penetrating 6 feet through the shingle to reach fresh water and nutrients.

They're not often seen, these communities of plants growing straight up from the seashore shingle. There are plenty of shingle beaches in Britain but most of them are too much hammered by the twice-daily tides. Beyond the reach of the waves there is often development and the well-meaning disturbance of sea-gazing humans. Most of Britain's vegetated coastal shingle is in East Anglia; it's a habitat unknown outside Northwest Europe, Japan and New Zealand.

And here's an enthralling paradox: it's the plants that make the plants possible. The plants themselves create an environment in which plants can grow: stabilising the shingle, depositing nutrients and encouraging more growth. Their success brings in animals that can feed on them, and they are followed in turn by animals that eat the plant-feeders. In other words, life begins with plants.

It's a real struggle to grow on Orford Ness. A plant can only grow in shingle that is comparatively immobile, and which contains finer material that can trap water and nutrients. The plants have to be capable of resisting drought: by storing water and letting it go with great reluctance, as a cactus does. These shingle plants get plenty of rain, but no sooner has it fallen than it's gone: nothing that you can walk on drains as fast as a bank of shingle. But there are plusses. The first is the shortage of competition: very few other plants can cope with such a difficult place, and so the small community of plants have the place to themselves. And if you choose these bleak places to live, there are very few things around to eat you. Large grazing mammals, whether wild or tame, do not seek out shingle banks, and small mammals and invertebrates are scarce.

But I wasn't in the mood for working out the Darwinian percentages as I sat on the shore at Orford Ness. I wanted to sentimentalise these fine plants: to call them brave, valiant, resourceful, indomitable, all the qualities you need to rise above the awfulness of war. But after a while, as I sat among the yellow horned poppies and the sea pea and the sea kale, I realised that this was wholly inadequate. It wasn't about moral qualities: it was about the fact that life loves to live; that life lives to make life; that wherever life can happen it happens and that wherever life can continue it continues.

I knew that as never before as I sat there on the verdant shingle: not as an intellectual fact but as an essential truth, something I felt in my essential guts. Then, after a while, I walked back towards the ferry that would take me to the Sailor's Arms on Orford Quay and the journey home. Thinking about bombs and death and origami cranes and the unbelievable inventiveness and tenacity of life.

And it always begins with plants. Without plants we would not be. Without plants, no Bach no Joyce no Shakespeare no Bashō no Barbara Hepworth no Darwin no Newton no Einstein no lion no tiger no cat no dog no porpoise no blue whale no crane no egret no bee no ant no butterfly no me no you.

I knew then that I was a bad botanist. And that I always had been. Just like everybody else.

Bluebell

2

YOU'RE BETTER THAN YOU THOUGHT

There's rosemary, that's for remembrance.
Pray you, love, remember.

Shakespeare, *Hamlet*

We take a terrible pride in our ignorance. In some ways we define ourselves by our areas of ignorance: in the belief that it's a modest, charming and amusing assertion of identity. An intellectual boasts about ignorance of sport, a scientist about ignorance of art, Richard Dawkins about ignorance of theology. People are delighted with their own ignorance of poetry or philosophy or physics or cookery or carpentry or classical music or soap operas or natural history. In the fourth form we had to choose between art and science and were invited to despise those who made the opposite choice. Our ignorance made us superior to those with knowledge.

If we can't know everything, we prefer to know nothing: we don't want to be an amateur, a half-arsed enthusiast. Perhaps it dates from the beginning of the age of television, when we could all invite experts into our homes. We will never be as good as them, so don't try: delegate knowledge to the expert on the telly. Total ignorance is cool. The dilettante approach died – well, perhaps at the end of the Second World War, when the work on Orford Ness became still more deadly.

I was happy to say it: I know nothing about plants. I'm a birder: trees are interesting because birds perch on them; all plants are interesting because they create habitats and all birds live in habitats. I look to the heavens for the soaring falcon; botanists are on their knees staring at the base earth. Mere stoopers.

Then I went to Orford Ness and realised that my ignorance was not only silly, it was phoney.

I didn't know nothing about plants; I was better than I thought. I knew the difference between a patch of grass and a Christmas tree, and that's a botanical distinction. I could also distinguish between a field of corn and an oakwood. I could tell a tomato from a grape. I knew quite a lot about plants; it was just that I had never realised it. We all do – how could we not? Seeing as we owe our existence to them.

There is a tendency to think that botany is about telling one wildflower from another. That seems rather a specialist thing, and perhaps – perish the thought – a little bit girly. Botany is immeasurably bigger than the names of flowers, both as a scientific subject and as a philosophical concept, but OK, let's humour this erroneous way of thinking. Let's name some flowers. And you can do it for yourself without any assistance from anyone because you too are better than you think.

Not all of us can walk through the countryside confidently identifying lady's bedstraw, ragged robin, navelwort, ivy-leaved toadflax and bladder campion. But I'm willing to bet you can identify getting on for a dozen wildflowers. I'm going to bet that you're already a bad botanist.

1. Primrose

Plants that flower early do our hearts good, bringing hope in dark times. Primroses are the *prima rosa*, the first rose of spring, weeks and even months ahead of real roses. They first appear in sheltered spots, five yellow notched petals, low to the ground, glowing, as if lit from within, in sunken places tucked away from the wind, or woodland clearings. As the year advances you find them in more exposed places, on roadside verges and railway embankments.

They have been much cultivated for formal municipal planting and for less regimented cottage garden use. The domesticated forms are called primulas; the scientific name for primrose is *Primula vulgaris*. These domesticated primulas come in fancy shades of white, red, brown, purple and deep blue, and are bred to flower much longer than the fleeting and fragile wild plants.

Primrose seeds have a funky method of spreading themselves: they delegate the job to ants. The seeds come with a fleshy attachment rich in protein, an elaiosome. The ants take the seeds into their nests where the elaiosome is consumed by the ants, but they don't damage the actual seeds. An ant colony depends on good hygiene for its viability and so the nibbled seeds are tidied up by the workers, away onto their rubbish tips, which also contain ant-droppings – frass – dead ants and other unwanted items. This provides a rich compost in which the seeds can sprout.

As early flowerers, primroses are a rich source of nectar to the pioneering insects, the first to show in spring. Queen bumblebees wake up from their winter rest (diapause) and fuel up on nectar straight away, so they can establish a nest and lay the eggs they have been carrying since the previous year.

2. Wild rose

We are all familiar with cultivated roses: wild roses are the same, only wilder. Much wilder. Instead of lush flowers with dozens of petals, sometimes never opening beyond the tightness of a bud, sometimes apparently modelled on a multi-coloured cabbage, wild roses tend to have five artlessly arranged petals, which can range through deep pink to pure white. You can find them in hedges when they haven't been flailed to bits, roadsides and many semi-wild places, growing on straggling, clambering, prickly stems, each one telling us complex things about the differences between wild and tamed plants.

There are about 300 species of wild rose worldwide, fourteen of them native to Britain. The most common of these is the dog rose *Rosa canina*, and it's a plant you will see all the time in late spring and summer, once you've got your eye in. When the flowers have gone they produce fruits in the form of rosehips, famous as a source of vitamin C, and much used for that reason during the Second World War, in an effort to keep the nation's children healthy. When I was at primary school in the 1950s, tapioca pudding with rosehip syrup was served at least once a week.

Roses have been selectively bred for human pleasure for at least 2,500 years, and there are thousands of different cultivars, some as different from a wild rose as a chihuahua is from a wolf. But just as both of these are essentially doggy, so hybrid tea roses and the dog rose of the country lane are both rosy.

3. Daffodil

We all know daffodils: bright yellow trumpets that you come across when you're walking lonely as a cloud. They're significant flowers for that reason: William Wordsworth's poem, first published in 1807, was revolutionary. It celebrated a beauty that was wholly wild: not cultivated, not part of a garden, nothing to do with the hand of humanity, growing for its own sake, to please no one.

Daffodils are also much cultivated, of course. The lane where I live is in springtime full of daffs, each one with a vivid orange trumpet: a cultivated variety got out and gone feral. There are seventy-four species of daffodil and a good 26,000 cultivars. (We'll talk about the difference between these two things later.) They're wonderfully easy to grow, leaping up from a bulb, and sprouting eagerly again the next year, so long as you leave the greenery to die back in its own time. (So if you have daffodils in your lawn, mow round them.) Most of them have their origin outside the British Isles.

But the plain ordinary daffodil, more lovely than any fancy cultivar and sometimes called Lent lily, has a good claim to be a native British plant. It was once far more numerous, but can still be found in those sudden colonies that give so much delight. These days we don't need to be told that there is beauty in nature, that nature brings us beauty beyond anything that humans will ever come up with. It's finding it that's the problem – but a host of golden daffodils will always help us to keep despair at bay.

4. Snowdrop

Snowdrops flower in Britain long before the spring equinox: little white bells coming up in defiance of the winter. The plants have hardened leaf tips that enable them to push through frosty ground, sometimes apparently taking on the snow in a whiteness competition. In some places they flower in a great mass and counterfeit a snowfall. They're much loved for their earliness, and also for the apparent modesty of their bearing: lowering their heads as if embarrassed by their beauty. They're associated with virginity for that reason.

Snowdrops are probably native to the milder south and west of Britain and Ireland, but they have been widely introduced elsewhere, as much for their symbolic power as for their earliness and prettiness. They generally flower in time for Candlemas, 2 February, which is the feast of the purification of Mary after the birth of Jesus. They have been much planted in ecclesiastical settings for that reason: virginal flowers which are now found growing wild all over Britain.

Like daffodils they spring from bulbs. Most cultivated

snowdrops are sterile but can propagate themselves by dividing the bulb. The chances of snowdrops producing seeds in
Britain are low: the flowers have mostly gone by the time
pollinating insects appear. We'll look at the relationship
between flowers and insects later on as well.

5. Cow parsley

In the English countryside in May, every lane, every field
margin, every path's edge is frothing white: uncountable
flowers, often abuzz with insects. This is the stuff to which
we give the rather dismissive name of cow parsley, as if the
plant was unworthy of our attention. My mother preferred
the name Queen Anne's lace, but it's all the same stuff: plants
apparently immune to the depredations of humanity.

The flowerheads are spoked like umbrellas. Plants of this
type are lumped together as umbellifers; both words come
from the Latin for sunshade. They are all, a little unexpectedly, members of the carrot family. There are a good few
plants that look a lot like cow parsley, with the same brolly-
like structure; these include hogweed, hemlock, fennel, wild
carrot, wild parsnip and ground elder. This family provides
humans with plenty of good nutrition, but it also includes
poisons that can irritate the skin (giant hogweed) and others
that can kill you (hemlock); more on these in Chapter 23.

We tend to celebrate the rare and take the common for
granted, but the exquisite sculptural quality of the cow
parsley flowerhead, the countryside-wide sea of white and
the Maytime bonanza of nectar are worth celebrating for
their own sake. A bad botanist is always ready to revel in the

commonplace, not least because it's so much easier to find. And identify.

6. Clover

Clover is familiar to us as a little cream globe rising from a casually managed lawn on a slender stalk; often we see this stalk bent almost in half as a bumblebee makes an ungainly landing on the flower to sup nectar. There are about thirty different species of clover native to Britain: some white, some pink, some red.

Their leaves are almost as familiar as the flowers, each one split into three leaflets, a trefoil. We all know that a four-leaved clover is lucky: for that reason, many a bad botanist can recognise clover without needing to see the flower; to be technical we can recognise the plant in its vegetative state. One leaf in 5,000 bears four leaflets. Some have even more: there's a record of fifty-six.

Clovers are members of the family of legumes, which includes peas and beans. They have the excellent effect of fixing nitrogen into the soil rather than depleting it, which makes them a helpful crop to grow if you wish to avoid excessive use of synthetic fertilisers. Clover is generally grown with ryegrass as a fodder crop; it's then fermented with the grass to make silage. Clover makes rich eating for herbivores: that's why a cow or a horse consuming it with relish is 'in clover'.

7. Daisy

Daisies evolved their way of life to survive the attentions of grazing mammals; they live on in millions of gardens all over Britain because the same strategy allows them to survive the attentions of lawnmowers. They exist as a flat rosette very close to the ground, easily missed by a munching mouth or by a spinning blade. They throw out their starry little flowers, yellow centre surrounded by white rays, at regular intervals, and even if these get munched or slashed away, they can always make more. There's scarcely a month of the year in which you can't find a daisy flower.

The name is a contraction of day's eye, which is a reference to the sun (Shakespeare referred to the sun as 'the eye of heaven'). The flowers close up at night and open up again the following morning, and they track the sun through the course of the day. Lawn fanatics fight daisies with ferocious chemicals, but in most back gardens people are content to let them have their way: a lawn starred with daisies is a pleasant thing in many eyes. I wonder: do children still make daisy chains?

8. Dandelion

The bright yellow discs of dandelion flowers seem an almost insolent proof that the human domination of nature is not yet complete. They grow up, bright and bold and ostentatious, in lawns, flowerbeds and roadsides, sprouting even from cracks in the pavement; and from the most uninspiring a beginning, they can produce these luxuriant flowerheads. (What we refer to as a dandelion flower is actually many tiny flowers all together – we'll look at what makes a flower in Chapter 5.)

We know dandelions just as well when the flowers have given way to seedheads: each seed that makes up the delicate little sphere is ready to float off on the smallest puff of wind or human breath, rising on its tiny parachute to land and, if all goes well, grow into another dandelion. As with daisy chains, I wonder if children still blow dandelions clocks, telling the time from the number of breaths it takes to despatch every seed into the air.

Dandelions were once grown for winter salads, prized for their ability to flush out your kidneys; one of their vernacular names is jack-piss-the-bed. Dandelions were considered especially good to eat if you were suffering from gout after overdoing the port. The whole plant is edible and nutritious; the leaves can be eaten in a brown bread sandwich and the roots stir-fried with nuts. (See Richard Mabey's superb *Food for Free*.)

9. Bluebell

As good botanists will make a pilgrimage to find ghost orchids and red helleborines, so bad botanists – good ones too – will make a pilgrimage to a bluebell wood in May. It's one of the great sights of the British countryside: dappled sunlight coming through the brand-new leaves on the trees to dapple the great lake of blue that lies beneath.

Bluebells are shade lovers, though they become flowers of open country out in the wetter west. They come in an astonishing range of shades of blue, all as subtly placed together as something from the brush of Claude Monet. They make one of those sights of inescapable beauty, beauty that requires no education, little experience and no idea whatsoever of what constitutes good and bad taste: like a rainbow, like a kingfisher ... and you wonder whether such flowers are beautiful because that's how we humans choose to see them, or whether they are beautiful for a reason – whether their beauty itself is some kind of survival mechanism. And that, of course, is another thing we'll be looking at later on.

10. Buttercup

A good botanist will point out that we lump at least three species together when we talk about buttercups: creeping, bulbous and meadow buttercup. There's an inevitable clash between folk taxonomies – the easy, intuitive and traditional way that a bad botanist understands the plants all around – and the scientific taxonomies that require pinpoint accuracy. We'll look more closely at that sort of thing in Chapter 21.

Buttercups are a dazzling bright yellow: five shining petals that reflect the light. One more children's game: you hold a flower beneath your friend's chin, and if you see a patch of reflected yellow on the skin you know your friend likes butter. The creeping species has tenacious roots and will grow in lawns when given a chance, and once there it is hard to remove – should you want to do so absurd a thing.

The meadow species is much taller, and often seen in big numbers in well-grazed fields. A folk tradition says that they make butter yellow, but in fact they're poisonous to cows.

They won't eat them, which is why you sometimes find them in big numbers in what's called unimproved pasture: pasture not treated with selective herbicide. They're also poisonous to us humans, but you're unlikely to eat enough to do yourself damage – they taste very bitter and blister the mouth.

11. Poppy

Poppies have a smart strategy for survival: the tiny seeds they spring from are long-lived and can hang about in the soil for many years and remain viable, and when the ground is disturbed, they germinate. Two ways of disturbing the ground: regularly ploughing it and regularly blowing it up.

Thus the red poppy is traditionally associated with cornfields and with the great battles of the First World War. The corn associations are mostly a thing of the past: the use of herbicides has chased them from the crops. Poppies can still be found on roadsides and, with more enlightened farmers, in margins around the field.

Traditions linking the poppy with death and new life can be traced back as far as Ancient Egypt: their blood-red obviousness makes that inevitable. But they were adopted as a fund-raising tool after the First World War and became a cherished and these days slightly ambivalent symbol both of that conflict and of British patriotism.

12. Water lily

One of the great events of history was the departure of

some plant species from the watery lives they had evolved for. They found a way of living on land, and that made it possible for animal species to live on the land as well. Some animals – which we now find in the forms of seals, whales, manatees and so on – later went back to the water. And so did some plants.

Water lilies are easy to recognise: flowers of unapologetic beauty growing right on the top of the water. They have waxy leaves, like the yellow horned poppy, though they have developed this trait to keep water out rather than to keep it in. These leaves are filled with air-spaces, so they float. Two species of water lily are routinely found growing wild in Britain: the white and the yellow.

They can cope with depths of up to 5 metres, 16 feet; the leaves are attached to rhizomes – an underground stem capable of producing both roots and stems – in the mud at the bottom of lakes, ponds and slow-moving rivers.

So there you are: a dozen flowers that most bad botanists – including most people who have only just become aware of the fact that they are bad botanists – can recognise without need for any reference material. You may be a bad botanist, but you're not as bad as you thought. We are always absorbing all kinds of information about all sorts of different things without knowing that we're doing it. Plants are everywhere – they're part of everybody's lives, whether you're taking a short cut through the park, driving through the suburbs or eating a meal. You know more than you think.

Daisy

3

HOW TO EAT THE SUN

And before you let the sun in, mind it wipes its shoes.

Dylan Thomas, *Under Milk Wood*

Let there be light.

That's how it all begins. Not just the Bible but life itself. Light doesn't just make it possible for us to see: it makes it possible for us to eat, to breathe, to exist. It makes it possible for us to think and love and dance and sing and go to the moon and make the *Goldberg Variations*, *Starry Night*, *Ulysses* and *The Origin of Species*.

Light does all these things, but it needs a middleman. The middleman is Plantae: the kingdom of plants. Plants are the intermediaries between us and the sun. Everything that lives is either a plant or depends on plants. There are exceptions when it comes to certain forms of microscopic life, but for practical purposes that principle is as sound as anything in the universe. Lions and tigers depend on plants every bit as much as horses and cows, and so do all fungi. (Old-fashioned classification divides life into three kingdoms: animals, plants and fungi. More recent taxonomies are far more complex, some versions containing, for example, twenty-eight kingdoms of bacteria. But the old-fashioned classification is good enough for a rough-and-ready understanding of life; in the same way that Newtonian physics is a helpful way of understanding the mechanisms that operate the Earth, even though Newton's theories have been superseded by those of Einstein.)

We are bad botanists. We are studying plants. Not just the wayside flowers, but the entire kingdom of plants: the vast worldwide empire of life-possiblising plants. Plants are the only living things that can eat light. Everything else that lives must eat light at one or more remove: the pride of lions that knocks down a buffalo gathers round to feast on the animal that ate the plants that ate the light; with white carnassial teeth and bloody muzzles the lions share a banquet of light.

The toughest carnivores on Earth are as dependent on plants as the gentlest vegetarians – and all because of light. Almost every traditional form of power comes from plants, directly or indirectly. We burn wood, we burn coal, which is fossilised plants, and we burn oil, which is the fossilised remains of plankton, some of which is plant (or plant-related) material, and some of which fed on those plants.

The great airliners that carry us from one end of the Earth to the other, the missiles that cross the skies in times of war, the car that takes you to the shops, the light that you switch on when it gets dark, the warmth that stops you dying in winter: all these things still mostly come from plants. And it's all about light. Plants, in short, are the only living things that can exploit and store the energy of the sun.

That's why plants are green and that's why green is the colour of life and that's why we talk about the green movement and the Green Party and being green or, if you are the former prime minister David Cameron, green crap. Green is the colour that addresses the light: green stuff is what makes the energy of light accessible first to the plants and then to plant-eaters and then to carnivores; green is what makes it possible for us to burn fossil fuels. The process of devouring light is called photosynthesis: the word means bringing everything together by means of light.

Plants take in light by way of chlorophyll: the green stuff. Chlorophyll exists in chloroplasts, which you find inside plant cells. It takes in the energy from the light and uses it to convert carbon dioxide and water into glucose; the plant takes in carbon dioxide through its leaves and water through the hairs on its roots. The plant doesn't eat light directly – it uses the energy from the light to make its own food. No light, no food.

This food created by plants is available to many other forms of life. Not that plants are keen on sharing the results of their photosynthesising brilliance. Many go to a great deal of trouble to avoid being eaten: roses have thorns, buttercups are poisonous, daisies lie low and yellow horned poppies flourish in places few herbivores can reach. Across millions of years plants have evolved ever more effective defensive systems and plant-eaters have evolved ever more ingenious ways of getting around them: it's an arms race that will carry on for as long as life continues on the planet, and we'll look at it in more detail in Chapter 23.

Photosynthesis is nearly as old as the planet. The Earth was formed 4.6 billion years ago; a little more than a billion years later there were photosynthesising bacteria in existence. They used hydrogen for the crucial business of finding a source for electrons. But in the course of the next billion years, these living substances found another way of doing photosynthesis. Instead of using hydrogen they used water. Water, as we all remember, has the chemical formula H_2O: that is to say, to each molecule of water there are two atoms of hydrogen – and one of oxygen.

Oxygen, eh? So what do plants do with the stuff once they have taken what they need from water? They dump it. They excrete it into the atmosphere. The waste product of a plant is oxygen. Which is not the worst news for those of us who belong to the animal kingdom.

Plants push out oxygen as a casual by-product of the way they make their own food. This seems little short of miraculous. I am reminded of the Babel fish in Douglas Adams's *The Hitchhiker's Guide to the Galaxy*: this is a fish that feeds on brainwave energy and then excretes it – so if you put one in your ear, you can instantly understand anything that's said in any language. *The Hitchhiker's Guide* itself comments: 'Now it is such a bizarrely improbable coincidence that anything so mind-bogglingly useful could have evolved purely by chance that some thinkers have chosen to see it as a final and clinching proof of the *non*existence of God.' This passage is followed by some brilliant quasi-theological logic-chopping.

And indeed, for us animals the excretion of oxygen is a thing of glorious and – should we wish to think that way – purposeful wonder. Plants breathe out oxygen and we breathe it in: what could be more simple, more glorious and more benign than that?

It was a catastrophe. The event is referred to by that exact term in some scientific works: the Oxygen Catastrophe. Oxygen built up in the atmosphere and the shallow seas and to many forms of life, it was toxic. Species that had existed and thrived across countless millennia suddenly found their world uninhabitable and that led directly to the extinction of many species that lived an anaerobic life. It's generally agreed that there have been six major extinction episodes in the history of life on Earth: the last but one, 65 million years ago, came about with the meteor that landed in the Gulf of Mexico and did for the dinosaurs; the sixth is going on right now. The Oxygen Catastrophe isn't included in this list, perhaps because it had such obvious benefits to the life forms that survived – the lineage that led to the establishment of the animals and therefore ourselves.

But it was a catastrophe all the same. Many life forms were snuffed out in a breath of toxic oxygen – and the world was left to the survivors, as is always the way with mass extinctions. We, the survivors who get to write the history, sometimes prefer to talk about the Great Oxidation Event, as if it was an unambiguous good. But there is no good and no evil in the process of evolution: only what is. Evolution has no goals other than to produce living forms that survive long enough to produce viable young: in short, life forms capable of becoming ancestors. Remember that point: it's going to crop up again and again, as it must when your subject is life. The organisms that could survive in a world full of oxygen were not better or more virtuous or singled out for greatness: they were just lucky.

And the luckiest of them all were forms of green algae that outperformed the red and the brown kinds. And 750 million years ago, there were at last plants that could live on land: mosses and liverworts.

But it didn't stop there, as we'll see in Chapter 18. The great rumbling unstoppable juggernaut of evolution just continued rolling along, eventually producing not just bad botanists but vascular plants over which bad botanists could botanise. Badly . . .

Hazel

4

THE CASE OF THE BAD BOTANIST

What a lovely thing a rose is!

Sherlock Holmes, in *The Naval Treaty*
by Sir Arthur Conan Doyle

I'm a bad birdwatcher as well as a bad botanist; the difference is that I'm a *good* bad birdwatcher. So when I pick out the song of a blackcap from a springtime chorus of garden birds or call attention to the silhouette of a sparrowhawk soaring above, I am used to a little faint admiration. *How do you do that? I wish I could do that.* And it's easy. Anyone can do it – once you have made birds an area of personal concern. That's a bird – and it matters, it matters to *me*. It's my business. Once it's become personal, everything else follows. I can't not notice a nice bird. It would be against nature. Some would call it obsession; I'd prefer to look on it as a passionate engagement.

The first Sherlock Holmes short story is *A Scandal in Bohemia*. The author, Sir Arthur Conan Doyle, needed to establish the singular nature of his hero in the opening paragraphs without boring those who had read the two Sherlock novels already published; ideally, drawing them in still closer. He does so brilliantly and economically. The story begins with Watson, who moved out of their Baker Street lodgings in the second novel, paying a chance visit to his old friend and flatmate. Holmes at once dazzles with a series of brilliantly accurate deductions about Watson. It's a virtuoso performance and Watson laughs in delight.

'I am baffled until you explain your process. And yet I believe that my eyes are as good as yours.'

'Quite so,' he said, lighting a cigarette and throwing himself into an armchair. 'You see but you do not observe.'

At this point I must go into confessional mode. My old friend Ralph (rhyme with 'safe', not 'Alf') is a *good* bad botanist. He once told me: 'You look at nature like a cat. You don't notice anything unless it moves.' Or makes a noise, I protested. And to tell the truth, I quite liked the idea of being a cat, self-contained, elegant, sphinx-eyed, walking by myself on my wild lone, looking at birds when they moved, responding with my agile feline brain to their sounds. And sublimely unconcerned with the unmoving plants.

I knew what trees were all right: birds perched on them and made nests in them while their leaves fed caterpillars and birds ate the caterpillars. Trees were thoroughly useful things: 'Marsh harrier! Coming out from behind the big tree!' I knew that in season a cuckoo often sang from a particular tree behind my house – no idea what kind of tree it was. So far as I was concerned, plants were an acceptable background, the chairs and tables and beds and the soft furnishing of the wild world. I knew intellectually that plants made every other form of life possible, but I didn't feel any emotional connection with them.

Oh, there had been moments, of course there had: leaning on the buttress roots of a rainforest giant, discovering a tamarisk glade in a hollow in the Namibian desert, sitting in the shade of a strangler fig in the Luangwa Valley in Zambia – or closer to home, ducking below the level of the seedheads in East Anglian reedbeds, coming suddenly upon great clumps of thrift on the Cornish cliffs and of course the fleeting, eternal bluebell woods. But I didn't think that plants were my business: they were for somebody else to worry about, somebody else to enjoy, somebody else to understand.

Silly really. I have always loved wildlife, but I saw but failed to observe the wild living things that make every other kind of wildlife possible. I had expanded my personal universe from birds and mammals to butterflies and then to other forms of invertebrate life, so it was a logical step to promote plants from the background to the foreground – and after my Atom Bomb Epiphany, I had no choice. When the pupil is ready, the teacher will come, say followers of Zen: my botanical enlightenment came when – or perhaps because – I too was ready.

And I was aware of three things at once. The first was that my area of ignorance was colossal. The second was that colossal though my ignorance was, I had a way in: I had acquired a certain degree of knowledge simply by being alive, as represented by the dozen flowers of Chapter 2. What's more, I had just identified a yellow horned poppy. I wasn't, as I feared, starting from scratch. No one is. And the third was that I knew it would be easy to expand my scanty area of knowledge. All it took was the will. I lacked it one day: next day I had it. Like love.

Plants were now an area of personal concern, so I started to notice them. Many years ago I bought a small motorbike, and all at once I noticed bikes: bikes everywhere, all different kinds of bikes, ridden by all different kinds of people. I had not known bikes had undone so many. It was something of the same thing when I realised that I was a bad botanist.

Now I noticed that there were plants everywhere and I knew the names of very few of them, but just enough so I didn't get completely lost: daisies and dandelions and so forth. So naturally, the first thing I wanted to know of each unfamiliar plant was the name. It all starts with names. Just knowing the name is a start, the only start, and it's a good one. Of course, it doesn't finish there, any more than your relationship with your neighbours ceases to develop once you know that they're called John and Louise. But a name is an essential start.

The best way to find the names of wild things is to spend time in wild places with someone who knows more than you. I have taken many a good walk with Ralph; he names the flowers while I name the singing birds. On a good day he too can distinguish between reed warbler and sedge warbler by ear alone, and I can occasionally tell a fleabane from a dandelion. I can call on Ralph even when he isn't there: these days most of us carry in our pockets more computing power than the Apollo 11 astronauts took to the moon. I can see a nice flower, take a picture, examine it later and when I'm baffled, a matter of routine, I can send it to Ralph for his views.

I ran into a problem at once: many flower names are unfamiliar and so they're reluctant to stay in the mind. It's all very well to be told that this one is 'sheep's-bit scabious', it's quite another to see the plant next time and say, ah yes, sheep's-bit scabious, I'd know them anywhere – pretty, rather fluffy blue flower. But hear a plain fact: one of the crucial skills in seeking after any new skill is self-forgiveness. It's all right to make mistakes, it's all right to get it wrong, it's all right to forget the name you've heard three times already, it's all right to have absolutely no idea what the damn thing is even after you've looked it up in three different books. That essential rule counts double when you're dealing with the wild living things: the reason you are doing so, whether you have articulated the thought to yourself or not, is biodiversity – a fascination with the way that life operates by coming up with many, many, many different kinds of living things. Every moment of bafflement is a joyous understanding of what biodiversity actually means.

There are six species of reptiles native to Britain. There are fifty-nine species of breeding butterflies. There are about one hundred species of mammals (including humans). A birder with more than 400 species on his British list is doing very well indeed; if you can manage even half that you're doing OK. And in Britain and Ireland there are about 1,500 species of native wild plants, including trees, shrubs, grasses, sedges, rushes, ferns, horsetails and what we loosely refer to as 'flowers'; more on that in the next chapter.

That doesn't include mosses, lichens and algae; it also doesn't include the plants we have domesticated and imported, either for food, for fuel, for fodder, as raw materials or to decorate our open spaces, and it doesn't include the species that we brought in from overseas, which got out and went feral.

You're never going to know all 1,500 of those natives. Crash-hot field botanists get puzzled on a routine basis: I've seen them at it, making a botanical survey. They come across something funky and they're as puzzled as hell – and that's a good thing. An exciting thing. They take a picture, make notes, and if they can't work it out on the spot, they look it up when they get home. They also make mistakes ... and that means that every bad botanist has a God-given right to make them too. No shame in mistakes, only in falsifying your data: that rule is as good for a bad botanist as for a good one.

As you become a slightly less bad botanist, you begin to make sense of the places and the times you walk through. You begin to get the hang of their patterns and rhythms. You also become more aware of the beauty and diversity of the world you live in. As you acquire more knowledge, you become better at observing. But the first step is the important one: realising that the relationship between you and any plant you come across is now a personal matter.

When we were at school, Ralph and I used to argue about books. He was for D. H. Lawrence, I was for James Joyce. So here, partly as a tribute to Ralph, is something from *Women in Love* that has always stayed in my mind. The characters are looking at hazel catkins, and Birkin has just pointed out the tiny red female flowers that grow on the trees, where they receive the pollen emitted by the long, dangly male catkins.

'Had you noticed them before?' he asked.

'No, never before,' she replied.

'And now you will always see them.'

That seems to me a kind of magic. Here is something that was always there and you never saw it: now you have noticed it once and from that moment it will always be there. It doesn't feel like a change in perceptions, it feels like a radical alteration to the external world: as if you had, by an effort of will, made the world more wondrous than it was before.

And it's what happens when a bad botanist becomes a slightly better botanist.

Sunflower

5

WHAT DO YOU MEAN, FLOWER?

I must have flowers, always and always.

Claude Monet

We all know what we mean by the word flower: so much so that we hardly notice that we routinely change its meaning with effortless ease and total disregard for contradiction. It doesn't matter: we know what we mean from the context and the tone of voice. A good botanist will be rather more precise: a daisy is not a flower but a flowering plant, and what it bears at the end of its stalk is not a flower either. It's an inflorescence or flowerhead made up of many very tiny things called – flowers.

When we talk about flowers in conversation, we sometimes mean the flower itself, as distinct from the foliage. But we give someone a bunch of flowers, rather than explaining that it's a bunch of herbaceous foliage with flowers (or flow-erheads) attached. A flower garden has much more than flowers in it, but the flowering bits are what matters. We refer to many growing plants as flowers, but only when they're actually in flower. Many wild plants (like daisies) are called flowers or wildflowers, as if their leaves, stalks, seeds and roots were irrelevant.

There are two ways of talking about plants. The first is with everyday conversational language. This is not only imprecise – it's also riddled with confusion. Many plants have several different common or vernacular names. Quite often these names are borrowed at random from other plants, plants not closely related: ground ivy is not close kin to the ivy that climbs up trees; lilies – sometimes referred to as true lilies – aren't closely related to water lilies or, for that matter, lily of the valley, daylily, arum lily, Lent lily and maybe a hundred other plants that get called lily. These folk names and folk taxonomies are a little tricky to get your head round, but they reflect centuries of fascination with plants and especially with their flowers. If you seek precision, scientific language is available, and so are scientific names. I'll attempt a little more clarification in Chapter 21, but the best idea is to live with the confusion and rejoice in it: because it's all a celebration of human engagement with biodiversity – and that, after all, is why we're here.

So it's all a little imprecise, but usually clear enough because we know what we mean when we're saying it: 'What lovely flowers!' It would be a trifle pedantic to say, when presented with a bunch of sunflowers: 'What lovely stalks and leaves and inflorescences!' But there's one thing we're certain about: flowers are quite different from trees, from the crops we see in fields and from the vegetables we grow and cook and eat. Informally, of course, we're quite correct. But technically we're quite wrong, and we need to get that straight in our minds if we are to be slightly less bad botanists.

In the film *Withnail and I*, the eccentric Uncle Monty wears a radish in his buttonhole and grows allotment vegetables in his sitting room in exquisite art nouveau pots. 'I think the carrot infinitely more fascinating than the geranium,' he says. 'The carrot has mystery. Flowers are essentially tarts. Prostitutes for the bees.'

But the carrot, like the geranium, is a flowering plant, related to cow parsley, as we have seen. Most plants – about 80 per cent of all species – are flowering plants. That adds up to around 300,000 species. If you fail to pull your carrot at the right moment, when the edible root is at its best for size and flavour, it will carry on growing and next year it will produce flowers: rather attractive umbellifers, as it happens. You can find wild carrots in flower along roadsides in the summer; most of us would write them off as more cow parsley, though the flowers are denser and perhaps prettier. The central flower in the cluster is often red: a red bead in a froth of white. Perhaps you've never seen such a thing before: now you will always see it.

Flowering plants are called angiosperms because the seed comes in a container. (The word comes from the Greek: sperm is seed, obviously enough; angio is a container or vessel. Conifers are gymnosperms because they have unclad seeds; for the Ancient Greeks, a gymnasium was a place where you went naked. If you've ever cooked with pine nuts, in salads or making your own pesto – by whizzing together pine nuts, olive oil, basil and parmesan – you'll have noticed that you don't have to shell the nuts; they come to you naked and unashamed.)

But almost all vascular plants are angiosperms. (Vascular plants have an internal plumbing system that transports liquids through its tissues, and that makes them different from mosses and liverworts and so forth.) So the grass on your lawn and the grass beneath the feet of the cricketers at Lord's, the footballers at Wembley and the tennis players at Wimbledon is a flowering plant, or rather, many flowering plants. Those at the sporting venues at least will never actually produce flowers because the groundkeeper's mower is relentless, but if they left off for a season, Centre Court would become a knee-high savannah of swaying flower-bearing plants. The flowers wouldn't be gaudy and only a good botanist would notice them. That's because they have no need to attract a living animal: they are pollinated by the wind. This might seem a little random and so it is, but grasses tend to grow close together and it's no great thing for the male pollen grains to find a receptive female organ nearby, especially if the plant produces a lot of them. Birches and oak trees operate the same way, usually over much greater distances.

Uncle Monty was right in that flowers are about sex, but not all flowers need bees. Flowers are an essential part of the angiosperm's mechanism for bringing sperm and eggs together, but to make things confusing for a bad botanist, many flowers have both male and female organs, though not all: some are either one or the other. A typical flower will have four whorls. The outer ring is the sepals, which are supportive. Inside that is the corolla of petals. The next ring is the stamens, or male organs, which produce pollen, and inside that, the pistils or female organs. A pistil has a stigma: the point at which the pollen – male – will operate. Flowers are symmetrical: either radially symmetrical like a starfish or a sunflower, or bilaterally symmetrical, like a human or a snapdragon.

So let's go back to D. H. Lawrence's catkins, and the flowers you will now always see. The hazel carries male and female flowers on the same tree (so it's monoecious). The catkins are male flowers, obvious and dangly and broadcasting pollen to the winds in huge quantities, in the hope that at least some of it will find the female flower of another tree. The tiny female flowers, which look more like buds, have red styles, which are part of the pistils – so here are two things that few people would call flowers, and yet flowers they are and they exist so that hazels can have sex and make more hazels.

If you haven't read *Women in Love*, you can be excused for failing to notice a female hazel flower. It doesn't matter to the tree if not a single member of the animal kingdom notices it. But it would be a disaster for many flowering plants if their flowers were overlooked. It would end any hope they have of becoming an ancestor. Many flowers are attractive: because they are designed to attract.

And at this point we had better take a brief Darwinian digression. By designed, I don't mean designed by a designer: I mean urged into being by the all-pervasive power of evolution. The teeth of a lion, the limbs of an impala, the tail flukes of a blue whale, the wings of an albatross, the deadly fart of a beaded lacewing larva that can kill six termites with one blast, the height of a Californian redwood, the sting of a nettle and the beauty of a wild rose all came into being from the forces of natural selection. So did your brain. Anything that gives an edge and makes it more likely for the owner of that edge to survive, prosper and become an ancestor is good: when that edge is passed on to the next generation, those that possess it in still more useful form will have a greater chance of becoming ancestors themselves ... and on and on and on, across the uncountable millennia, until what is produced looks very much like purposeful design but is in fact the result of a billion billion chance occurrences.

Many flowering plants are pollinated not by wind or by water but by animals, often enough bees, as Uncle Monty said. And the thing that gave them their edge and continues to give them their edge is beauty. Or to be less contentious, their power to attract. The song of birds is beautiful, their alarm calls are not. Birds sing to attract mates: song is *supposed* to be gorgeous; it wouldn't work if it wasn't gorgeous, at least in the ears of its target audience, which is female birds of the same species. Flowers are beautiful, roots are not. Many plants produce flowers to attract visiting animals: they too are *supposed* to be gorgeous. We humans are not the target audience of either blackbirds or roses, but both fall within what we might call the human arc of gorgeousness. We respond to their purposeful beauty: sometimes by making music of our own in imitation of the birds, sometimes by wearing flowers and by giving them as gifts, sometimes, like Claude Monet or Henri Matisse, by painting pictures of them, sometimes by planting them in places where they will give most pleasure and looking after them so they grow better. We have been doing some or all of these things for a million years.

A flower, then, is a way of getting sperm, found within the pollen, to the ovule, which contains female reproductive cells. The great snag in being a plant is that you can't move from one place to another, so when it comes to sex you must delegate the moving-about part. Most plants need external help: wind, as we have seen, is one solution. A few water plants use water. And very many flowering plants get animals to do the job.

But no animal would take on the job of being middleman in plant sex out of sheer benevolence. What's in it for me? The first answer is nectar. This is a liquid rich in sugars. The plant makes nectar, at considerable energy cost to itself, and offers it in flowers. Nectar provides energy to those that consume it. It gives many insects the power to fly on. It's also great brain food. Nectar is a brilliant resource for many insects in their adult form. Butterflies did all their serious eating when they were caterpillars, but while they are adults, constant topping up with nectar powers their brief lives and allows them to find a mate and, if female, to lay the resulting eggs in an appropriate place. Many insects seek out nectar: it's not only good stuff, it's easy to find. Nectar-drinking has been taken up in a big way by many species of mosquitoes, hover-flies, wasps, bees, ants, flies, midges, beetles, butterflies and moths. They arrive, sup nectar and then fly on: as they do so, they accidentally (at least on their part) pick up a dusting of pollen. They then fly on to another flower and lo, the pollen is transferred. The ideal result occurs when the insect in question travels to a different plant of the same species, and when they land to take on further refreshment, the pollen is transferred to the new flower: the sperm reaches the egg, the plant can reproduce and the globe can keep on working.

Pollen is itself good stuff, and not just from the plant's point of view. It is good nutritious food, with more body to it than nectar. It follows that many animals are eager to eat it. Pollen-eaters are technically palynivores: a good number of species, including many bees and ants, take pollen into the nest (or hive) to feed the larvae. If that wasn't in the flower's initial gameplan it is now: many flowers overproduce pollen and so, as the palynivores move from bloom to bloom, they leave a few grains behind at each stop. Bees will take some nectar for their own use, so that they can keep going, but their main job is to collect pollen and bring it back to the hive for the grubs, the next generation. Plenty of pollen makes it to the hive, but enough of it gets transferred to the female parts of flowers of the right species and all is well for both. Thus the plants exploit their own predators.

And if all that seems rather chance-dependent, so it is. What odds would you give on any one insect collecting pollen, carrying it off, landing on the right receptive flower – same species, different individual plant – and successfully transferring the grains to the female parts? Not something to bet the house on, is it? But if you toss a coin again and again and again, you will get results that seem impossible in isolation. A run of, say, a dozen heads in a row is highly unlikely in a sample of twelve tosses, but it becomes a stone-cold certainty when you toss your coin a million times.

Which brings us to one more question (for now). How do you, a flowering plant, get a pollinating animal to pay you a visit? You offer a reward, yes, fair payment for the job. But also you have to let the animals in question know that you've got something worth having. So you advertise. You put up a wanted poster and wait for the bounty hunters to arrive. That's not what flowers are for, but it's why so many flowers are gorgeous. They don't just seek to please themselves: their future – as potential ancestors – depends on pleasing others.

There are two very effective ways of advertising and many plants use both. The first is scent, which carries a powerful come-hither message that many insects can pick up from improbable distances. The advantage of this method is that you don't have to see the plant to know that it's there and offering something good. Some plants release their perfume as the sun falls, a fact that gardeners sometimes exploit to create night gardens. But the function of such nocturnal smells is to attract night-flying insects, most obviously moths.

Most flower scents are reasonably attractive to humans, some emphatically so: people have been wearing the scents of flowers on their bodies for many thousands of years. Others are less sexy. A classic example is the rainforest monster called rafflesia, which stinks of the death and putrefaction of mammals. That's because its target audience is carrion flies, which come expecting a bonanza of rotting meat and operate as inadvertent – and duped – pollinators. For a still gaudier trick see Chapter 24 on orchids.

The second and more important summoning signal is of course appearance: shape and colour. The plants are competing with each other to be the most attractive to pollinators. They compete between species and they compete within species. But they also cooperate: a sumptuous flowering meadow is hugely attractive to large numbers of potential pollinators and once an insect has arrived, the plants compete among themselves for the attentions of the bees and the butterflies: survival of the gorgeousest.

'Endless forms most beautiful and most wonderful ...' – words from the last sentence of Darwin's *The Origin of Species*, and this is more obviously true of flowers than of anything else that lives. Flowers have evolved uncountable ways of being beautiful and wonderful and we don't appreciate the half of it, as we can see in only three colours. We can't see into the ultraviolet part of the spectrum but many insects can; many flowers, as a result, glow in ways invisible to us, sometimes making a fully lit landing-strip to guide the insects down their flightpath onto and into the waiting flower.

In the warmer months flowers are with us all the time and almost everywhere, even in cities. There are stands of flowers in railway cuttings and on motorway verges. Flowers crop up wherever there's half a chance of life. What could be more ordinary than the lane that leads from my house, and the banks that rise modestly from either side? My thoughts turned to those banks as I turned to *The Origin of Species*. The last paragraph begins: 'It is interesting to contemplate an entangled bank, clothed with many plants of many kinds . . .'

So I pressed 'Save' on my keyboard and set out to walk to the end of the lane and back, a journey of perhaps half a mile in total. My task would be to contemplate an entangled bank, especially its clothing of plants, especially the flowers, and to put a name to as many of the plants in flower as possible; plants that a more experienced and accomplished botanist would pay little heed to. I set out to celebrate the absolutely ordinary, with the naive eye that is the glorious privilege of the bad botanist: something that the good botanist and the non-botanist can only envy.

Cow parsley

6

THE ENTANGLED BANK, PART 1

I know a bank where the wild thyme blows.

Shakespeare, *A Midsummer Night's Dream*

Our house is at the end of the lane, which rises gently through as much as 20 feet in the course of a quarter-mile, because we are at the bottom of what we in Norfolk humorously call a valley. There are six houses on it, no through traffic but a fair few comings and goings. The shallow banks on either side generally get mowed once a year, in high summer by a council sub-contractor, when the vegetation threatens to meet in the middle. There is farmland beyond on both sides: grazing meadow at the bottom and arable fields nearer the top, so the banks get a liberal dose of agricultural run-off, mostly fertilisers. The plants that grow here are, then, liberally dosed with nitrates and exhaust emissions. In other words, this is not a special place, not something a good botanist would campaign to preserve or spend a lifetime studying, unlike the lightly grazed floodplain on the valley floor, which is indeed a little special. So I would like to stress that the plant community of this little lane, of these two opposed entangled banks, is about as ordinary as it gets.

It was May. The daffs and the snowdrops had gone – we were on to the next stage. So off I set: the bad botanist in action, marvelling both at my own ignorance and my own knowledge, unsure which was the greater marvel. I was also confident that my knowledge would be greater by the time I had completed the journey and done all the looking-up.

1. Cow parsley

As mentioned before, most of us can recognise cow parsley. But is it OK to like the stuff? That's a difficult question. For a start, it's ubiquitous: May and June roadside verges in countryside and the wilder suburbs are a great sea of frothing white; cow parsley is so commonplace that it's almost easier to despise it than to pay close attention. The plants feel like weeds and we have an atavistic response to the very idea of weeds: weeds being plants we don't want. There's an archaic term, tares:

> *Give the angels charge at last*
> *In the fire the tares to cast!*

Words from a harvest festival hymn. Weeds are sinners, destined to be burned while the righteous prosper. We tend to resent certain plants, and these plants are usually vigorous, commonplace and persistent. Does that include cow parsley?

Cow parsley likes agricultural run-off: it thrives on the excess nutrients that leach into the soil from the crops. A good botanist will – rightly – resent the fact that these chemicals allow cow parsley to thrive – and thrive – at the expense of many other species. We manage our countryside in a way that promotes the commonplace above the special, and that's a sad thing.

But cow parsley is a symptom of this problem, not the cause, and if we take a moment to look at it, we can see the plant's virtues: the way it grows fast and tall, annually seizing control of time and place in the advancing spring. It functions well in shade, being both tough and versatile, a winning combination in the human-dominated world. As I walked along the lane, a male orange-tip fizzed past, a butterfly that always operates in the most terrific hurry. I wasn't getting distracted from my botanic assignment by my traditional fascination with things that move (well, maybe a bit) because cow parsley is a favourite nectaring plant for this species: small butterflies of mid-spring, mostly white, but the males carry, as the name suggests, orange flashes on the tips of their wings. Cow parsley is a good strong early nectar source for many other species, especially butterflies and hoverflies. Rabbits like their feathery leaves.

And the flowers are not without beauty in their own right. Look at one in isolation – try a close-up picture on your phone, to take it out of context – and you will see that the flowers (flowerheads) are really rather exquisite. The plants are, as said earlier, related to carrots, celery and parsley; they have been used to treat stomach problems.

These days they are quite often selected as cut flowers, to give a little informality to a bride's bouquet or a mildly rustic touch to an arrangement in a vase, setting off the more luscious blooms that we have domesticated for human delight. We value wildflowers more than we used to, and appreciate a less formal kind of beauty.

2. Nettle

This is not a plant that we readily refer to as 'a flower', but nettles are flowering plants and, what's more, they were just coming into flower as I walked the lane: discreet strings and blobs of greeny blooms. They are perhaps the most resented plants in Britain, sprouting up everywhere and causing an always surprising amount of lingering discomfort when we brush against them. We should admire them for that: their robust defence system means that grazing mammals leave them alone; they thrive in fields where everything else has been grazed to the ground by our cattle and our horses.

We may not love nettles but nettles love us. They are the great camp followers of humanity: a rich array of nettles is always a strong hint that humans have used this place. Nettles like disturbed ground and enriched soil: human settlements leave ashes, bones, the droppings of domestic animals and middens for human excrement – and the nettles leap up in joy as a result. And like cow parsley, nettles love agricultural run-off: lanes in farming country tend to be dominated by these two plants, telling us – shouting – that in this place we put humanity's interests first. Or at least, what we believe are humanity's best interests. There are a few living things that can take advantage of the human-centred world, and we usually despise them for it: rats and nettles love us, but we seldom love them back.

But nettles once played an important part in our year: they are among the first edible green plants to put their heads above the ground in spring, and they're a rich and important source of vitamins A and C. People plucked them with joy, relief and stout gloves: fresh food at last after a winter of living only on what could be preserved. Cooking nettles removes the sting. They are also the food plants for the caterpillars of many of our favourite butterflies: red admirals, small tortoiseshells, peacocks and painted ladies. Every garden should have a nettle-patch – and it's not as if it's a challenging crop to raise. The lane was dominated by cow parsley and nettles, but there was plenty of other stuff there too, and I didn't have to look too hard to find it.

3. Garlic mustard

This is different from wild garlic, which springs from a bulb and has thick, fleshy leaves: garlic mustard is a tall plant which can reach a good metre, with heart-shaped, rather nettle-like leaves, but these are hairless and don't sting. Crush them in your fingers and you get a faint aroma of garlic and mustard. They were in flower as I walked: modest flowers big enough to do their job and no more, the sort of wildflowers we easily overlook because we're more used to the massive blooms of the plants we cultivate for their flowers. These flowers were small and white, shirt-button size, four petals to a flower, arranged in a cross: a triumph of understatement. They have the nickname jack-by-the-hedge, because that's where you find them – happy in the shade. Sometimes I think it's worth becoming a bad botanist just for the names.

Humans have relished garlic mustard for centuries, often as a flavouring for lamb or fish; we liked it so much we took it to the New World, where it has become invasive. They are biennials: that is to say, they have a two-year life cycle. The flowering plants I saw were last year's; the young plants don't show above ground until September, and that's the best time to harvest the leaves. I'm told you can use them for a nice pesto, even though they contain cyanide; the cyanide dissipates when the leaves are chopped up. Apparently.

4. White dead-nettle

They're called dead-nettles because they look like nettles but don't sting. What's the point of that? Grazing mammals are apt to leave them well alone, just to be on the safe side. Just as many hoverflies look like wasps but don't sting, so dead-nettles look like nettles but are equally stingless.

When these plants flower, they look less nettle-like: above the saw-edged leaves there's a neat column of white flowers rising up the stalk, looking like a set of beads. They are inaccessible to many species of pollinators, but to others, equipped with long tongues, they are just what's required. By narrowing their target audience, these plants ensure a devoted following: white-tailed bumblebees are regulars, and so are red mason bees. It's also a favourite food plant of the caterpillars of the gorgeous garden tiger moth. Adult green tortoise beetles specialise in this plant: small insects that really do look rather like tiny green tortoises.

It's said that country boys used to pick dead-nettles and chase the girls with them, pretending they were stingers. And they too have a fancy name: Adam-and-Eve-in-the-bower. If you turn the plant upside down and look at the flower, the gold and black stamens look like two human figures stretched out in bliss. Who'd have thought it?

5. Dandelion

No surprise to find this one by the side of the road, and no kudos in recognising it, but dandelions are of more interest to the very good botanist than you might think because of their tendency to vary. They are in the genus *Taraxacum*, which contains thirty-four species, but among them there are reckoned by some to be more than 2,000 microspecies; and there are 235 of these in Britain. If you are capable of recognising a single one of these, you have already gone beyond the scope of this book – and if you're not, you can take a moment to reflect that what we're talking about on every page of this book is diversity. That's what entangled banks – like every other wild habitat on Earth – are all about.

Dandelion stalks give out a milky fluid when you break them, as some of us will remember from childhood. This is sticky and there have been many attempts to use the substance to make rubber. The Germans did what they could to develop the idea during the Second World War, for fears of being cut off from the rubber suppliers, who were mostly in Asia. Attempts have continued and, in 2014, Continental developed a prototype rubber tyre made from dandelions.

6. Red dead-nettle

This is a lot like the white dead-nettle except the flowers are red instead of white – a pinky sort of red rather than robin-bright. They too like disturbed ground – it's amazing how often this phrase comes up in descriptions of our most common plants. We humans have disturbed an awful lot of ground: good news for the few who like it that way, bad news for many others. But come – today we are revelling in what we've got.

The leaves are notably hairy and nettle-like, but carry no sting. The flowers come early, sometimes even in February, and can be found into November. At both ends of the year, but especially at the start, they are an important nectar source for the long-tongued species of bumblebees. They are also a handy source of pollen early in the season, when queen bumblebees are raising the first brood of the year; the grubs, pollen-fed, will grow up to become the workers that feed subsequent broods, allowing the queen to concentrate entirely on egg-laying.

7. Daisy

Here's another deeply familiar plant. It has another name: woundwort. Daisies were once gathered in sackfuls before battles, and bandages were soaked in their juices. These were applied to sword and spear wounds. In fact, a good few plants have the name of woundwort, and were used in a similar way.

8. Bluebell

Not the great blue lake that spreads across a woodland floor in that treasured way; on the Entangled Bank I came across single plants poking their heads up here and there. Bluebells spring from bulbs. Bulbs aren't roots; they're modified underground stems that contain fleshy overlapping leaves, as everyone who has ever chopped an onion knows.

Bulbs are food stores: resources that allow the plant to survive over winter and leap into action as soon as the weather changes. Bulbs aren't like seeds: they are good-to-go mature plants, and can produce flowering stems from the same bulb year after year. But there's a payback to this strategy, as there is to every strategy. A bulb with its stored food is a suitable food item for many animals, and down there in the earth it's available to the rooters and diggers and snufflers. The champion forest snufflers are wild swine, more usually called wild boars, as if it was a species without females. It's been speculated that bluebell woods are a comparatively recent phenomenon, postdating the extinction of wild swine in Britain; they were finally hunted out by the seventeenth century. But in many places, most notably the Forest of Dean, they have made a return, a new wild population rising from escaped animals that had been kept for the restaurant trade. I wonder what that means for bluebell woods?

9. Ground ivy

I expect most of us have heard the name with a curse attached, because the plant annoys gardeners and is hard to get rid of. That's because it's good at spreading, doing so by stolons: horizontal stems from which flowering stems can sprout, thus the plants spread in clumps and mats. Attack it and the plant will rise again from broken stolons.

Ground ivy is not closely related to real ivy, the plant that climbs up walls and trees; it's a classic example of a random folk name, apparently chosen to confuse bad botanists and make them give up. Ground ivy is actually related to the dead-nettles, but it's not a convincing nettle mimic – so there's another piece of confusion this time by way of science rather than folklore.

The leaves are bright green and usually described as kidney-shaped, and they have small, neat purple flowers. The plants do well in shade or sun. Sometimes they are actively cultivated by gardeners in pots, and even as ground cover. They have been used to cure coughs, to flavour ale instead of hops and as a substitute for rennet (which comes from a cow's stomach and curdles milk) to make cheese. And they have some nice folk names: Gill-over-the-ground, alehoof and run-away-Robin. If you rub the leaves they give off a sharp smell; it's been compared to both blackcurrant and cat piss. It's all in the nose of the beholder.

10. Lesser celandine

These are natty little plants of the early and middle spring and they look like little suns fallen to earth: shiny green leaves close to the ground and just above them shiny yellow flowers, usually in small groups. They are named from the Greek for swallow, *chelidon*: nice if fanciful, for both species give warning of better times ahead. February 21 is known to some as Celandine Day: it was the day on which the great eighteenth-century parson-naturalist Gilbert White noted the year's first celandine. His great work *The Natural History of Selborne* has never been out of print, and is essential reading for anyone with a taste for nature.

It's very possible, perhaps even probable, that the lesser celandine affected your childhood. When my father was a boy living in Wigan in the 1930s, he loved the radio programme *Out with Romany*. Romany, real name G. Bramwell Evens, was the electronic media's first wildlife presenter. In response to this programme, my father wrote a letter to Romany saying that he had seen a lesser celandine, the first of the spring. His letter was read out on the programme: 'And Edward Barnes from Wigan . . .' It was a moment of intense joy.

So when my father went on to work for BBC children's programmes, television rather than radio, he resolved that the programmes should be driven by the audience and should include the audience whenever possible: children were not there to be preached at or kept quiet, they were there to participate. It was their programme. He put that belief into practice when he was producer of *Blue Peter*, and later when he established a number of new programmes, including *Grange Hill, Record Breakers, Multi-Coloured Swap Shop* and, most famously, *Newsround*, the first news programme for children.

It follows that when I see the first lesser celandine of the year, and when I find them in a quick stroll up the lane and back, I think of my father.

11. Buttercup

Buttercups are in the genus *Ranunculus*, which contains 600 species worldwide, so there's diversity for you. Some of them have been cultivated for gardens and for cutting. As said earlier, there are three common species in this country; this one was, I think, the lanky meadow buttercup. Other buttercup names: creeping crazy, devil's guts, old-wife's-threads, goldweed, soldier buttons.

12. Lesser stitchwort

Lesser stitchwort is another of those plants with modest flowers: flowers that are there to do a job for the plant, rather than to please humans. Getting an eye for this understated kind of beauty is one of the earliest rewards that come to the bad botanist. Lesser stitchwort has small white flowers, each of five petals, but the petals are deeply notched so it can look more like ten. They grow on the top of plants that can be knee-high and taller, so the flowers look tiny in this context. These flowers only last three days, but the plant keeps producing new ones. They're called stitchwort because they were said to cure stitch, the discomfort that comes from exercise.

13. Germander speedwell

It's worth becoming a bad botanist just for this: a common plant with a tiny flower. Instead of catching it in the tail of your eye walking by, you can pause for a moment and look down and admire: a small deeply blue flower with a white dot in the middle. They've been called 'child Jesus's eye'. They're supposed to bring luck to travellers: wear one in your buttonhole to speed you well on your journey. (Actually not such a great idea, since they fade very fast.) They are low growing, forming mats and patches.

14. Greater celandine

Just what you wanted to know: another plant that's not closely related to other plants with the same name. The greater celandine is not first cousin to the lesser celandine: just one more confusing name. Greater celandine is in the same family as poppies, which makes sense: much less showy, but with the same sort of flabby, rather untidy petals. They grow knee-high in the verges, and the flowers have four bright yellow petals, quite unlike the sunburst of the lesser celandine. The petals don't overlap, so you can't confuse them with buttercups.

15. Archangel

About five years ago I was walking down the same lane when I saw a flower I had never seen before. Correction: a flower I had never observed before. Ralph had been up for a visit, and wild plants were very much in my head and my floral eyes were operating better than usual. And so I stopped and I took notice, for this was a really rather nice little plant. It looked like a nettle, and in fact it's yet another dead-nettle, but that wasn't what struck me. It bore a generous spike of yellow flowers, like beads, at the top of the stalk, all mixed up with those notched leaves.

I looked it up when I got home and found without much difficulty that it was called archangel, or yellow archangel: the hifalutin name comes from the fact that it doesn't sting you; it looks fierce but is actually benign.

And it was a bit of a breakthrough. I had seen, observed, noticed, researched and named a wildflower, and Ralph can take only distant credit for this. I had established a personal relationship with the plant: it was now part of my brain, part of my thinking, part of the way I see the world. I had been walking this lane for five years, and all the while I had been entertaining archangels unawares. Now I always see them. It was a moment of confirmation: I had finally made it. Now I really was a bad botanist.

Dog rose

7

WHAT'S IN A NAME?

That which we call a rose
By any other name would smell as sweet.

Shakespeare, *Romeo and Juliet*

There's a scene in *Brideshead Revisited*, Evelyn Waugh's mad novel about love and infatuation and (or with) the aristocracy, in which Sebastian invites Charles to Brideshead, the fabulously beautiful family home. Charles is entranced.

'Is that dome by Inigo Jones too? It looks later.'
Sebastian replies: 'Oh Charles, don't be such a tourist. What does it matter when it was built if it's pretty?'

What does it matter what kind of flower it is if it's pretty? It's an unanswerable question. In one sense it doesn't matter at all. I have many times been rebuked with Sebastian's argument for my knowledge of birdsong: what does it matter if it's a song thrush or a blackbird, if it's pretty? Well, it may not matter to you but it matters to me. A name is not a label but a portal – walk through it and your understanding grows: of the individual, of the ecosystem it inhabits, of the world we all share.

And is prettiness enough? Is it ever enough? You might, for example, turn on the radio and out pops the aria *'Ich folge dir gleichfalls'*. You would be well within your rights to say, yes, indeed, a pretty song. You might even say, how much more than pretty. But it's also possible that the experience would be even richer if you knew that the piece was written by Bach, that it's part of the *St John Passion*, that the German words (for which I need a parallel translation) are about following with joyful steps, that the soprano voice is singing against two flutes, that both are kept in check by the ballast of the continuo, the bass part, and that the song is about following Jesus to judgement and death . . . so it's a very complex and nuanced joy that's being sung here. It's pretty all right, but not just.

It's my view that when you are powerfully attracted to something, knowledge and understanding will allow you to get in deeper and to find an experience more densely packed with meaning. And in any walk of life, the opportunity to get in deeper is available to us all. It's not about previous knowledge, it's about personal choice. Flowers are pretty and I have often looked at them and said yes, how nice – but I'm a good deal richer for my experiences with the yellow horned poppy and the archangel, both of which took me to a deeper level. Since I became a bad botanist, I seek the name, I seek the beginning of an understanding and I seek the beginning of a relationship.

So let's go back along the lane. How did I know that one was lesser celandine and that one was greater celandine? I am reminded of my old friend Manny Mvula, one of the first top-level Zambian guides to work in the Luangwa Valley. Back in the 1980s he was being interviewed for his guiding qualification by the old white guys who were then in charge of the safari industry. He gave, as is his wont, a dazzling performance. Eventually one of them asked him: 'How come you know so much?'

Manny smiled sweetly: 'I have read a lot of books.'

So that's where we start: with a lot of books. The first step towards greater skill in identifying plants – flowers, let us say for now, to keep things simple – is to look them up in books. The most useful thing you can do here is to identify the plant; the second most useful thing you can do is fail to identify the plant. You learn by looking, by trying and failing. You're allowed to fail.

And you will fail often enough because there are two main problems with flower ID books. The first is that they have so many flowers in you feel like giving up before you start; an excellent and brilliantly put-together book might give you getting on for 2,000 species.

That leaves an obvious gap in the market: for books for beginners, bad botanists for the use of. Books that don't acknowledge quite so many species. This is a great idea but the problem is that by cutting down so drastically – a couple of hundred species or even fewer – there's a very good chance that the flower you're trying to identify isn't in the book.

I have one such work here on my desk: it describes 150 species. At the same time it's both not enough and too much. It's hard to know where to start, it's boggling. So the first thing to do is to accept that (a) becoming a slightly better botanist is actually quite challenging and (b) you're not going to put a name on every damn flower you see. Accept both the difficulty and your fallibility and you've already taken a hefty step on.

Many guides to wildflowers are cannily organised and offer well-thought-out ways of identifying your plant. The problem is that most of us use such a book by the instinctive method of thumbing-through: riffling through the pages until you find something that looks vaguely right, and then narrowing your search. Most of these plant ID books are organised in a scientific way: that is to say, they group closely related species together. This is a good idea, but it's not unfailingly helpful to the bad botanist: those who are beginners, with an instinctive but unorganised understanding of plants based on folk taxonomies and personal experience. That leaves you, often enough, with the challenge of thumbing through the entire book, which is not easy.

Thumbing-through works pretty well if you're trying to identify a bird. If the bird you saw was a lot like a duck, the chances are you'll find it among the other ducks. It's not hard to grasp the fact that a duck is a duck, even when it turns out to be a small goose. But you'd need to be a moderately advanced student to assign a straggly wayside plant with yellow flowers to the cabbage family. We all know what a cabbage looks like, and it seems only fair for wild members of the cabbage family to look similar. But they don't. That rather leggy plant with those nice yellow flowers just happens to be wild cabbage, not to be confused with the similar wild turnip.

But when you think about it, these yellow flowers look

quite a bit like rape, the plants grown on vast English prairies for their oil content, which paint the countryside so bright and so yellow. It's not a great leap to accept these as brassicas, that is to say, members of the cabbage family. It's important to accept, right at the start, that the whole point of nature is that it's quite devastatingly complex: so we must now learn that the nice plants with purple flowers, the herby plants called honesty, are also cabbages. And it came as a mild shock to learn that a favourite plant of mine, the cuckoo flower, is yet another cabbage. These are damp-loving plants that flower about the time the cuckoos arrive; alternative name lady's smock. And while we're at it, the garlic mustard that added a little savour to the previous chapter is yet another member of the cabbage family.

So the advancement of botanical knowledge is about changing our assumptions and our rough-and-ready folk taxonomies into something a little more organised and scientific, and about accepting that nature is shockingly diverse, far more diverse than we ever dreamed until we started to look more closely. It's confusing, but look on it as one more aspect of the great adventure. I know, I know: we all want to understand botany better by means of a series of effortless intuitive leaps. We can do that all right, but only by doing a little homework. So let's start with books.

Books can give us information, but they can't impart familiarity. They can't, for example, tell us about size in a way that we can grasp with a glance. Colour of flowers is crucial, but no book can get it right every time: flowers vary, according to individuality, light and local conditions, and colour reproduction is never going to be perfect. The time of year a plant comes into flower is essential information and you will certainly find it in your book, but not in a way that you can grasp at a glance. This awareness of the calendar of plants is acquired by living through the seasons again and again, looking at the plants as you go. It's something I am only beginning to get the hang of myself: you can't imagine how proud I was to be able to write that stuff about cuckoo flowers, and how pleased I am to look for them and to find them when May is almost upon us and the cuckoo is calling in our shallow little valley. These days I see a cuckoo flower and say to myself: huzzah! I really am a bad botanist now.

So what are the best books? I asked my old friend Duncan Macdonald, founder of the excellent company WildSounds, because he knows. And for fat books he recommends *Collins Wild Flower Guide* (2nd edition). This includes grasses and trees, so it's pretty comprehensive at 704 pages.

The Wild Flower Key incorporates a binary key, which is more accurate than thumbing-through hoping for the best. It operates on a series of yes–no questions: if yes, move on to 31, if no, go to the next entry. Here is a great resource for someone with ambitions to become a better botanist.

Harrap's Wild Flowers is designed with the thumber-through in mind: there's a chequerboard of images inside the front and the back covers that together give you a possible start. The images, all photos, are very good indeed and the layout is clear and inviting.

The problem with trying to understand biodiversity is that life is so bewitchingly diverse. But there are helpful books for rank beginners, and they work so long as you accept that they have no aspiration to completeness. They are a huge help when you're gasping at diversity and hoping to find the correct name of the odd flower. Here are some recommendations from my own experience.

The Dorling Kindersley title *What's That Flower?* boasts that it's the simplest ID guide. That's because it's left out most of the species. It classifies flowers by colour: if you find a large yellow flower there's a decent chance that you will find it in the book under large yellow flowers, and if it's not a daffodil it might be a yellow flag. It's somewhere to start and I've found it very handy.

The *Larousse Easy Way Guide: Wild Flowers* has only a few more species and invites you to identify them by means of a clear binary key. 'Does each flower have a long narrow spur?' If yes, it's fragrant orchid, if no, you go on to another question. It's a book that teaches you how to look.

It's all about pattern recognition. You need to feed these patterns into your brain for later use, and you do that by looking at plants and at images of plants. One of the best ways of doing that is by putting up charts and Duncan recommends a good few. Examples: *Guide to the Flowers of Walks and Waysides,* also *Guide to Ancient Woodland Indicators.* You can buy them – and plenty similar – for a few quid and Blu-Tack them up in appropriate places for contemplation: for the subtle and almost unconscious accumulation of patterns and information.

But there's an important principle to take on board before buying your books: they don't work unless you read them. Purchasing them is not enough. ID books are a bit like diet books: you acquire them full of good intentions but something inside your mind tells you that once you've paid for them, further action is unnecessary. You will gain the information or become thin without any more effort, just as last year's purchase of a language primer means that you now speak perfect Spanish. Alas, such books can only open the door: you have to walk through by yourself.

Books are essential, both for identification and for the beginnings of an understanding of what you have identified. And then of course you can use those new-fangled computers. The website www.wildflowerfinder can give you very helpful information, and it can be used by experts and beginners alike. You can click and find information about what type of plant you see (tree, shrub, unspecified flower and so on), colour of flower, number of petals, month of flowering, type of flower, stem shape and so on, and then you press go and the engine will rumble away and come up with a suggestion. It's not a straightforward business for beginners, who are not yet looking at things with a good botanist's eye. For example, it's easy to count the petals of lesser stitchwort at ten; as we've already seen, when you look more closely you see that there are only five, each one deeply notched. Take careful notes as well as careful photographs and you increase your chances of coming up with the right name. This website can give you answers and it also helps you to train your eye and your mind. It's a very good piece of work and not at all intimidating.

There are also apps for smartphones that will do a very great deal of the legwork for you. Or have a damn good shot at it anyway. You use Pl@ntnet by taking a photo of your plant – just the leaf will do in many cases – and then asking for a search. You can also use the Google Lens function on Google Photos: you take a picture of your plant – or anything else – and the machine will try and tell you what you're looking at.

It's important to remember that the names they come up with are suggestions. Neither app is infallible. One of them told me that a greater celandine was a marsh marigold: I knew better because I could see it wasn't standing up to its waist in water and the phone couldn't. And sometimes there will be no answer, or no useful one. (I have found Google Lens particularly good for insect ID, which is great, but beyond the scope of this book.)

Is it cheating? Well, no doubt those who learned the names of plants by word of mouth considered those new-fangled books a form of cheating. But the fact is that knowledge is not the same thing as sport, unless you choose to make it so and hold a quiz. Anything that advances knowledge seems to me a good thing.

But with the simple click-photo-click-name business, I think it's important to remember that the name is, as always, not the end of your search but the beginning. When my clever machine gives me an apparently correct answer, I try to make a point of reading up a little more, about the nature of the plant and its comet tail of folklore, by looking the plant up in my books and/or on the internet; often information pops up unprompted on my phone as a result of the search. A favourite resource here is Richard Mabey's *Flora Britannica*. The aim of plant ID is not just to find the name but to invite the plant into your life, so you will know it next time and have the beginnings of an idea what it means. Thus plants take root in your mind.

Blackberry

8

TUTTI FRUTTI

You shall know them by their fruits. Do men gather
grapes of thorns or figs of thistles?

Matthew 7:16

The ambition of every flower is to be fertilised. The purpose
of every fertilised flower is to become a fruit. All flowering
plants produce fruit – every single one of them: apple trees
and orange trees, grasses and oak trees, roses and lesser
celandines, cacti and water lilies. A fruit is a device for the
protection and subsequent dispersal of the seed or seeds it
contains. It's the seed-bearing structure of a flowering plant,
and it's formed from the ovary when the flowering is done.
You can't always eat them but they're fruits whether we like
it or not.

So once again we have two worlds in collision: the world
of science, which deals with the way plants actually work,
and the everyday world of easy assumptions, folkloric

classification and the way plants *seem* to work. We all know
what a fruit is: it's something full of sugar that's good to eat,
especially as a pudding after the major nutritional tasks have
been completed: apples, strawberries, grapes, rhubarb, pears
and figs. And fair enough, they are indeed all fruit – apart
from rhubarb, which is a leaf stalk, technically a petiole.

You might have encountered other fruit on the same
dinner table a little earlier in the proceedings: aubergines,
tomatoes, courgettes, runner beans, mangetout peas, sweet-
corn, butternut squash, pumpkin, peppers and chillies. In the
informal language of the kitchen, we call these vegetables
and put them in the same category as potatoes (tubers, or
stored underground food reserves) and onions (bulbs, modified plant stems) and spinach (leaves).

We traditionally understand many (perhaps all) plants in a
rough-and-ready what's-in-it-for-me sort of way: often on the
basis of if and how we can eat them. Tomatoes are obviously
fruit: in Italian they are *pomodori* or golden apples and they
have the traditional nickname of love apples. But we don't
think of them as fruit, and that's because we eat them with
the main course rather than the pudding. (Old line: knowledge is knowing a tomato is a fruit. Wisdom is not putting it
in the fruit salad.) But if we are to advance our understanding
of botany, the kitchen is a good place for learning, not least
because it dramatises the mental jump we must make if we
are to become slightly-less-bad botanists.

The rice in the store cupboard is technically a fruit, or
many fruits. That's not a helpful notion for a cook, but it's
an important idea for a botanist. A grain of rice is not an
entire fruit: the outer hull is first removed, and that gives you
brown rice, richer in minerals and fibre than white rice. Strip

away the bran layer and the cereal germ and you have white rice. The flour in the jar on the next shelf is made from the fruits of the grass species we call wheat: these are hulled and then ground up to make them easier to eat. You can then add liquid to make a dough. If you can bring in a little fungus – you can find it in the air and many other places – you can make leavened bread, for the fungus is called yeast.

The fungi you have in the fridge – in the form of edible mushrooms – may have been on the same supermarket shelf as the plant parts we have been discussing – tubers, bulbs, leaves and fruit – but in scientific terms they would be better off on the meat counter. Mushrooms, like all fungi, are consumers of plants. Only plants can make their own food: fungi need plants just like the cows, pigs and sheep people consume, and just like the people themselves.

But we were talking about fruit. Fruits follow flowers. After fertilisation has taken place – the pollen shifted from one plant to another by wind, by water, by bee or beetle or bat – a flower changes. The anthers and the stigma wither and the petals drop off. The ovary enlarges and the ovules develop into seeds. Every seed contains the embryo of a plant.

It's a strange thing: when we say that something has gone to seed, or a place or a person is seedy, we mean nothing but bad things, when obviously going to seed is nothing less than the renewal of life. You could hardly imagine anything less seedy than going to seed. Going to seed is only a bad thing for a gardener: when a rose bush is producing fruit, its heady days of bloom are over for the year, so the garden is less beautiful, or at least, less showy. And if you forget to pick your lettuce it will put up a floral spike, and that will in time produce its own fruit, enclosing its seeds. A gardener who lets his lettuce get in such a state is no gardener: those in neighbouring allotments will pass by and suck their teeth. Meanwhile the floral gardener will pluck the dead heads off the roses so that the plants produce more flowers instead of fruit – though not all cultivars are so obliging.

Here's a way to revolutionise our understanding of plants: we look at fruit and ask what use it is to the plant itself, rather than us. So let's start with a wild fruit that's good to eat, one we have no hesitation whatsoever in calling a fruit: a blackberry.

Blackberries grow wherever they can. Unmanaged land is full of long prickly stems of bramble that sport jaunty white flowers. These turn into glistening black berries – though a good botanist would call them aggregate fruit composed of small drupelets. Either way, they offer themselves like caviar to the passing walker. The berries at the tip are the first to ripen, and they're the juiciest and loveliest on the stem; those behind follow more slowly and are better kept for pies and jam.

Blackberries are a unique survivor in modern Britain: the only plant that people in their thousands still forage for. Blackberries pass straight from wild land to human mouth as if we were still hunter-gatherers. Most of us have collected scratches – scars of honour – along with the berries; many of us have taken them home to make a genuinely atavistic pudding. But the plant doesn't produce these fine fruits to please us. A bramble produces blackberries for the sole purpose of making more brambles.

This can be explained by the family dog of my childhood, a collie-cross named Duff. She accompanied us on blackberrying outings and ate her share straight from the bush. She had a great liking for them, and in season would lag behind on more vigorous walks to take the fruit with a delicate nip of her carnivore's incisors. Blackberries often grow at a good height for a dog, and for a fox too: the keen-eyed (and keen-nosed) observer will in season find foxy droppings of a rich blackish-purple. Other mammals – dormice, squirrels and badgers – also eat blackberries, and many birds will take them as well.

The berries contain seeds that have a hard coating and are indigestible. But they're tiny: no big deal, they pass straight through. The eaters are unharmed by this experience – and so are the seeds. The consumers will dispose of the seeds by defecation, usually at some distance from the bush. That way the seeds get spread, with a nice dollop of fertiliser as a bonus.

As we all know, blackberries are not black and shiny from their first appearance. They start off green, hard and dull, not remotely inviting: there's no point in being eaten before the seeds inside the fruit are fully developed. Only when it's to the plant's advantage to attract the consumers do the fruits become delicious, and when they do so, they signal their deliciousness by changing colour. It's not enough to be edible: they must sell themselves, flaunt their edibility as the flowers before them signalled their stores of nectar and pollen. When Alice was in Wonderland, she found a cake that bore the words 'eat me'; a ripe blackberry sends out precisely the same message. Many fruits that seek consumers go through a flamboyant change in colour, and as they do so, they also become filled with sugar. They look delicious and they are delicious: an honest strategy that has ensured repeat customers across the millennia. Leave a patch of ground for three or four years and like as not you'll have a bramble there, and be able to pick blackberries from it.

The fruits that we refer to as 'fruit' in casual conversation have developed their edibility as an evolutionary ploy. They are delicious on purpose, just as many flowers are attractive on purpose. Their job is to be tasty: if they're not tasted, they've failed. The berries that fail stay on the stem and lose their tastiness. It's traditionally said that you should never eat blackberries after Michaelmas Day, 29 September – because on Michaelmas night the devil pisses on them.

Tastiness is not the only strategy available to a fruiting plant; we'll look at others in due course in Chapter 10. You will also note that many plants produce fruits that ripen and appear to sell themselves as extravagantly as blackberries, but they aren't all delicious. At least to us humans. Some are even poisonous; we'll save poisonous plants for Chapter 23. Let's pause here for the merely distasteful and look at the fruit of hawthorn trees: the (when ripe) bright red berries called haws. They are said by some to be just about edible, though no great treat. But we humans are not the target: haws are mostly eaten by birds. There is a potential evolutionary advantage in being more attractive to birds than mammals: birds can fly and so they're likely to carry the seeds further than a mammal could before they let them fall. Haws are a particular favourite of thrushes, most notably the thrushes that come to Britain for the winter – fieldfares and redwings.

My grandfather was a great gardener and he loved black-berries. All along the fences of his garden in King's Heath, Birmingham, he would grow blackberries: the ornamental plants – those cultivated for their flowers rather than their fruit – grew between the lawn and the blackberries. My grandmother would preserve the harvest every autumn: her kitchen and pantry were lined with huge purple jars, and every visit was celebrated with pies and crumbles that burst into royal colours at the touch of a knife or spoon. They were, as my grandfather seldom tired of explaining, not ordinary wayside blackberries: these were Himalayan blackberries. This is a different species, actually native to Armenia and northern Iran, one that gives larger and sweeter fruit. It was introduced into the country in the nineteenth century. Different cultivars of this species have been developed in order to make them yield even more fruit.

There are nearly 400 species of blackberry across the world: they're native to Northern Europe, Northwest Africa, Central Asia and North and South America. This is also a group that has a great tendency to diversity within a species: 400 microspecies have been found in Britain. Even the most obvious wild plants have a complexity we never dreamed of when, as children, we plucked the tip blackberry from a cluster, escaped a scratching, ate it – and rejoiced in the fact that it was a good 'un, and that there were plenty more where that one came from.

Honeysuckle

9

THE ENTANGLED BANK, PART 2

Gentle odours led my steps astray,
Mixed with the sound of water's murmuring
Along a shelving bank of turf . . .

Shelley, 'The Question'

It was the poppies that did it. You can't miss a poppy, and there were a good few of them growing on the Entangled Bank. So, though it was less than a month since I had last attempted to identify all the flowers on the roadside bank between my house and the top of the lane, I thought it might be instructive to have another crack at it. I was pretty optimistic: I reckoned with a bit of luck I – even I, a bad botanist if ever there was one – might be able to find half a dozen species that weren't in flower when I last did the brief walk.

I found sixteen. It wasn't even difficult. So here are the

new flowers from the first week of June, and it began with a bang – a few square feet of vertical hedge that were so crazy-full of flowers you could hardly see the green: delicate pinky-golden trumpets and a great frothing cascade of white foam.

1. Honeysuckle

This is a pretty familiar plant to most of us, even if we need someone to remind us of the name, because it's a garden favourite as well as a wild plant, much cultivated for its rich scent, especially of a summer evening (the scent pulls in many species of pollinating moths), and for its ability to climb over fences and, with a little encouragement, outbuildings. Look for crowds of cream-coloured trumpets that turn yellow-orange as they mature. I have a childhood memory of being shown how to pluck a single bloom and drink the nectar from the base.

There are 180 species of honeysuckle worldwide; in North America they attract hummingbirds. But we are concerned here with the most common British species, also known as woodbine.

> *Sleep thou, and I will wind thee in my arms . . .*
> *So doth the woodbine, the sweet honeysuckle,*
> *Gently entwist . . .*

That's Titania in *A Midsummer Night's Dream*, expressing her love for Bottom, who has the head of a donkey. The name of woodbine will get a small smile from those of certain age:

Wild Woodbine was the name given to a brand of notoriously cheap cigarettes, unfiltered and the great working-class smoke until the early 1960s: 'Light up life with a Woodbine!'

The plant – honeysuckle, not tobacco – grows wild in woods and along hedges and is the food plant of the classy white admiral butterfly. The berries, which appear later, are much favoured by dormice. Young girls were traditionally forbidden to bring honeysuckle flowers into the house, for fear that the heady scent would bring them lascivious dreams.

2. Elder

You might argue that this isn't a flower but a tree. Others will argue that it's not a tree either. And it can't be a bush because it isn't bushy. But elders are often found in and alongside hedges and are sometimes allowed to grow above the rest of them. It's a plant of forgotten places, often rather looked down on, but a rich and generous thing for all that.

There's an elder in one of Britain's best-loved paintings: it's growing alongside the house in John Constable's *The Hay Wain*. Elders were often planted hard by houses to ward off the devil – though some prefer the more prosaic idea that the plant helps to pull damp from the house. But elders have many powerful associations: in some Christian traditions elder was the wood from which the cross itself was made; in others it was the tree from which Judas hanged himself. There are magical associations to this day: followers of Harry Potter know the crucial importance of the Elder Wand.

The plant I saw was a thick mass of white flowers, which

would give way later in the year to deep black-purple berries. Elder flowers are prized for their flavour: you can use them to make a mildly alcoholic drink traditionally called elder-flower champagne. Wine made from the berries is said by some to be as good as a good claret. It's a plant rich in beauty, tradition and belief. Be careful with it: if you burn the wood, you will see the devil.

3. Rose

We have already talked about roses in Chapter 2, and will meet them again when we discuss the domestication of plants in Chapter 16, so I will be brief. The lane was in some places ablaze with roses, mostly whitey-pink and pinky-white, though some were still deeper in colour. There are four species of hedgerow climbers found frequently enough in Britain, but the one most often found is the dog rose, and that, I believe, is the only one in the lane. There are also a number of recognised subspecies and any number of hybrids.

Dog roses are good at hedges: the spines hook themselves onto neighbouring plants and this support allows them to reach good bright positions, wonderful for attracting simple human eyes or the compound eyes of pollinating insects. They can reach a decent height by this rather rough-and-ready climbing technique: beyond the hedge I could see them 4 metres high in a little spinney, and they sometimes reach 10 metres. The five-petalled flowers starred the hedgerows intermittently all the way up to the top of the lane: a classic example of an everyday miracle. You can see them as easily from train windows as along country lanes: in fact often better, for in many country places the hedges get flailed too often.

4. Poppy

I once played cricket on a ground with a thatched pavilion. On one side was a meadow with half a dozen shire horses grazing with quiet absorption, on the other a field of ripening wheat lavishly spotted with poppies. I felt as if I was playing in one of the idyllic Edwardian cricket matches of literature. Such fields still crop up in the British landscape, but only in places where herbicides are not used.

Poppies prospered in the cornfields of the pre-chemical era because their annual lifestyle fits in so well with cereals: they grow swiftly and they have flowered and set seed long before the corn is harvested, and they are pretty tolerant of non-chemical methods of weed control. The field poppy contains rhoeadine, which is a mild sedative. There are getting on for 132 species of poppy (in the genus *Papaver*); the opium poppy, not native to Britain, is *Papaver somniferum*.

5. Bramble

Bramble is used as a generic term for tangles of prickly vegetation and as a specific term for the blackberry plant. It was the blackberries that dominated along the lane, making intricate prickly walls with the dog roses, so that it seemed that a single plant was bearing two different kinds of five-petalled flowers, the brambles smaller, mostly white but a few shifting fetchingly into shades of pale pink.

A first-year bramble stalk, the primocane, can grow 30 feet in a single year but it won't produce flowers until the following year, when it becomes the floricane. The plant's rapid growth creates a network of prickles impenetrable to most mammals of a decent size, and that makes them very significant in the way a wild landscape develops. More on that in Chapter 14.

6. Mallow

Mallows are so tall and showy that you might think they were cultivated garden plants gone feral. There are a good few cultivated varieties, but the wild ones are dramatic enough: plants up to a metre and more high, flowers deep pink with purple stripes. The French name for mallow is *mauve*. They can bloom from June right through to autumn.

Mallows were probably introduced into Britain by the Romans, who rated them highly for their edible seeds and leaves. Many believed that the plant had other virtues as well. Pliny the Elder noted that mallow was considered 'a cure for all kinds of stings, those of scorpions, wasps and similar insects, as well as the bite of the shrew-mouse'. He also reported that in some people's view, a daily dose of mallow juice ensures that 'he will be exempt from all diseases'. He added that the plant was 'naturally adapted to the promotion of lustfulness'.

The Ancient Egyptians made a sweetmeat by mixing the

sap of mallows with honey, a treat for the elite. In eighteenth-century France, a similar treat was developed, mixing mallow root, honey and egg white. A related plant, the marsh mallow – which has bright yellow flowers, grows in water and is not to be confused with the greater celandine – could be used to make a still stickier sweet, and marsh mallows were much gathered in the Thames estuary, where they were then common. The sweet became so popular that it outran the easy supply of mallows and gelatine was used instead: it survives today as a marshmallow.

7. White campion

Some plants are dripping with human history while others just get on with the job of being plants, acknowledged in passing rather than acquiring a payload of folklore and meaning. White campions are cheery roadside flowers that out-compete many of their neighbours by pushing out a powerful scent at night to attract moths. They have five petals, white as you would expect, deeply notched so as to divide each one almost in two. Behind the petals there is an inflated sort of bladder, technically the calyx. As a result, the plant is sometimes called bladder campion, but there is a related species with the same common name, in which the bladder is even more pronounced. The plant is notably hairy; it's a perennial (coming up every year) but it changes its look as it ages, producing more flowers on forked stems.

8. Red campion

You can confuse red and white campions until they flower, and then they're unmistakable: five-petalled pinky-red flowers, also deeply notched, fusing into a calyx that's more like an urn than a bladder. They are geared to attract daylight pollinators, especially hoverflies. They grow in woodlands as well as along roadsides and tend to flower just after the bluebells, though sometimes the two coincide for a special feast of colour and drama. There are tales of campions protecting the honey stores of bees and keeping fairies safe from discovery.

9. Ox-eye daisy

Not a hard one to identify: they are just like the daisies in the lawn but big. They like roadsides and field margins – there was a time when I rode my horse daily round a vast field that was ringed in season with ox-eye daisies: each stalk crowned with a flower we know not to call a flower but a flowerhead or inflorescence, each one comprising a yellow disc of florets surrounded by between fifteen and forty white ray florets, which we know not to call petals. They have a number of good names, the best of which is moon daisy or moonpenny: in late evening light they seem to glow like little moons. They are also called dog daisy, field daisy and marguerite.

The name of ox-eye is descriptive: as a bovine eye looks unnaturally huge, so the daisy also looks like an oversized eye. Homer calls Hera 'the ox-eyed goddess' for the largeness and beauty of her eyes; she is the sister and wife of

Zeus, perpetually raging at (or horrifically revenging) his serial infidelities. She is of course beautiful (though Paris disastrously preferred Aphrodite), and so the epithet is a compliment.

The plant is associated with love and romantic divination, still to be found in the somewhat debased form as the game of 'he loves me, he loves me not', in which you must pluck off a petal – sorry, that's ray floret – at each repetition, hoping that you have selected an odd-numbered bloom.

10. Doves-foot cranesbill

This is a low plant with bright pink flowers the size of shirt buttons – and it's a geranium. Sorry to say this, but the plants we normally call geraniums are technically pelargoniums. We muddle the common names of plants with immense enthusiasm: we also muddle the scientific names when we aren't using them scientifically. The species here is *Geranium molle*; the flowers that we grow in pots and window boxes are usually a cultivated hybrid, for example *Pelargonium* x *hortorum*. That means we should rewrite T. S. Eliot's 'Rhapsody on a Windy Night' to read:

> *Midnight shakes the memory*
> *As a madman shakes a dead pelargonium . . .*

which doesn't scan but the idea's the thing, as all pedants will agree.

An odd thing happens when you start chasing information about these ultra-common plants of untended places:

it's often easier to find out how to kill them than how they live. Here's some helpful advice about doves-foot cranesbill in your lawn: 'For a large infestation, a selective herbicide will have to be used.' The human attitude to nature – or at least one aspect of it – is summed up for all time in the word 'infestation': take heed, humankind! One false step and our lawns will be infested with gorgeous little pink flowers!

11. White clover

If this plant's sweetness and inevitability are not enough to charm you, then I can point out that the trefoil leaves are gathered by wood mice and that they are also an important food plant for the common blue butterfly: that's the one that looks like a small shard of sky that has got loose on your lawn or roadside verge. I suppose that if we allow clover to grow all over the place there is a danger of an infestation of common blue butterflies, but perhaps we could learn to live with it.

12. Dock

Sometimes called bitter, butter, broadleaf and bluntleaf dock, this is another of those ubiquitous plants that we seldom notice. They were in flower along the lane, but the flowers aren't tremendously exciting: a spike of small greenish flowers that turn red as they mature. If we notice them at all, we notice the big, fat leaves.

These are traditionally rubbed on nettle stings as a cure:

when I was a boy, I thought dock was short for doctor. I have often heard that their alkaline sap neutralises the acid in the nettles, which is a lovely idea were it not for the fact that dock leaves are not alkaline. Other explanations exist: the evaporation of the sap cools the inflamed skin; they work as a counter-irritant; or that they are placebo, a botanical equivalent of kissing it better. But they are genuinely useful for wrapping up your freshly churned butter: the evaporation keeps it cool.

They can grow surprisingly tall in sheltered places. I remember Ralph and I coming across a colony of head-high docks in one of those narrow lost-world Devon combes.

13. Ribwort plantain

Another plant, another confusion: perhaps you thought that a plantain was a not-very-sweet banana used in cooked savoury dishes. So it is, but it's also the name of a group of common plants that we mostly overlook; the understated flowers on long stems that look like grasses. These stems rise from a rosette of pointy leaves, the usual term is lanceolate: an oval that develops into a sharp point, like the tip of a lance. These are marked with strong parallel fibres a little like ribs.

The flowerhead is like a dark brown egg wearing a white wreath, quite distinctive when you've got your eye in. These are or were used in traditional children's games: the flower-heads can be fired off as deadly missiles, or can be beaten off competitively in a game like conkers. The seedheads stay on the plants in winter and are a handy food source for goldfinches.

14. Foxglove

There was just one, standing a little behind a fence on an area of verge that had been kept short by my neighbours. It stood a good metre high, with its double-row of purple bells: a spectacular plant, much cultivated in gardens. Since this one wasn't in an actual flowerbed, I decided to count it as a wild one. After all, it's a fairly fabulous sort of plant.

There's a sweet idea that people once really believed that foxes wear the flowers on their paws to escape detection, but that's probably a retrospective fantasy. The name is more likely from folk's gloves: gloves worn by the little folk who must not be named, lest they bring bad luck.

15. Hop trefoil

I had never seen this plant before, or to be accurate, I had never observed it. It was a low clump of green leaves, triple leaves as the name suggests, punctuated by little fluffy yellows blobs a little larger than the sugar beads you use to decorate cakes. Each blob comprised a good few little blobs: if I'd been smarter I'd have made the connection and realised that it looked a little bit like clover and, indeed, is related to clover and makes good fodder. It's not closely related to hops but the flowers look a bit like those of hops, so one more confusing name. Anyway, now I will always see them.

16. Narrowleaf hawksbeard

There are a good few plants that look like dandelions and many of them are actually related to dandelions. Quite a lot of them are called false dandelions, which doesn't advance us much. Even I could work out that these weren't dandelions: too tall and they didn't restrict themselves to one flowerhead per stalk. These stalks – leafless, bar the odd straggler – branched near the top and each branch bore its own little sun: half a dozen and more to each main stem, like a candelabra. There's a pleasure in knowing its slightly funky name of hawksbeard, and an added pleasure in knowing these are not dandelions. So I allowed myself a gloat: ha! Only a *really* bad botanist would confuse a hawksbeard with a dandelion.

So there were sixteen plants, every one of them common and obvious: easy to ignore and almost as easy to invite into your brain. Sixteen! Here was a small but miraculous revelation of diversity. Just as well I hadn't delayed: on 10 June the council sub-contractors mowed the lot. Norfolk County Council says that their policy is to mow for safety, never for tidiness. I felt that some of this mowing was a little, ah, overzealous. I decided to walk the lane again in a week or so and see how the plant community responded to the trauma.

Dandelion

10

SEED DISPERSAL

But other fell into good ground, and brought forth fruit,
some a hundredfold, some sixtyfold, some thirtyfold.

Matthew 13:8

For us humans a fruit is something nice to eat: for a plant it's a stratagem for spreading seeds. As the great wooden horse was for the Greeks, so is every fruit – in the vast expanded notion of fruit that we considered in Chapter 8 – is to a plant: it's what's inside that counts because it makes victory a possibility. The function of a fruit is the most important thing in life: which is to allow life to carry on. The outcome of the plant's seed dispersal tactic determines whether or not the plant will become an ancestor.

Even bad botanists know that plants tend to stay in the same place. That can be helpful when you wish to check whether your hawksbeard really is a hawksbeard or some other species of false dandelion: you can always go back for another look, confident that it won't have flown away. Time-lapse photography has made it vividly clear that many plants are capable of movement and can respond to stimuli: the tendrils of climbing plants seem to lash themselves into a fury in their search for something to grasp. But we can accept the principle that plants don't move *much*.

But when it comes to spreading plant embryos – that is to say, seeds – movement is essential. If your own seed germinates bang next door to you, it's competing with you for the same resources. An acorn that falls under a nice big mature oak tree is unlikely to do much good: the parent plant is shading out the light, soaking up most of the rain and taking most of the available nutrients from the soil. The acorn will probably have a better chance somewhere else. There's a second advantage: a seed that travels a fair distance from its parent has an opportunity to grow in new places, opening up new worlds and new possibilities. You might scalp your lawn when the blades cut too deep going over a bump: the bald patch left behind is a perfect opportunity for one of those infesting doves-foot cranesbills.

Just falling off the parent plant is at least a start. That's movement, even if it's mostly downwards. Distance is not too much of an issue with short-lived plants – some of these live for just a few weeks, which means that they aren't in serious competition with their own progeny: the parent plant is already gone by the time its seeds have germinated. But even falling can be achieved with sophistication.

And an apple or a horse chestnut drops from its tree and, with a bit of a bounce and roll, some will get a decent distance from the parent tree, which is at the very least a good start, especially if they manage to land clear of the shade.

Buzz Lightyear in the film *Toy Story* is not, as the plot makes clear, a flying toy. But as Woody grudgingly admits, he is capable of 'falling with style'. Many plants produce seeds that fall with style. So let's look at the seeds of dandelions and sycamore trees, and see how they operate the Buzz Lightyear Principle.

A dandelion seed seems simple enough when you blow a dandelion clock: each one is lighter than a feather, it floats, it catches the wind and off it goes, eventually to land on some roadside verge, some clump of waste ground or someone's lawn and set off on its now-stationary journey towards the production of those bright yellow flowers (or flowerheads), followed by the dandelion clock: in other words, the fruit. And that's a parachute, that's obvious, isn't it? It has a heavier end, a stalk and a floaty, filmy top. But when you look closely, you'll see that the parachute isn't something you'd trust for your own descent from a dizzy height. It's not a closed canopy like a proper parachute, it's more like the spokes of a cycle wheel: surely not enough to arrest the fall of anything, even when it's as light as a dandelion seed. But those empty spaces between the spokes make a difference. As air passes through the spokes, it creates a vortex ring above the seed, and it's this ring of air, rather than the spokes themselves, that slows the descent of the seed. It's basically a parachute made of air, not attached to or contained by the seed's structure. Technically it's a detached vortex. And if you ask how a plant was able to think up such a thing, beautiful in both its simplicity and its complexity, then I will do my best to explain in Chapter 18.

In the same chapter I'll also try to explain the process that enabled sycamore trees to invent the helicopter – or at least

something intriguingly similar. Each sycamore seed pos-
sesses a single wing: an elegant shape that is even cleverer
than it looks. The weight of the seed is greater than that of
the wing, so it falls seed-downwards. The tip of the wing
is broader than the seed, so it catches the air as it falls. The
broadest part of the wing slows more because it's subject to
more air pressure – the pressure that comes from the descent
through the air. As a result, the whole thing starts to spin. It
autorotates. Technically that's because the centre of the mass
is in a different place to the centre of pressure. The seed acts
a bit like an axle: the almost-still point of the whole device
with the blade of the wing spinning rapidly above it, and this
spinning slows the fall drastically. A sycamore seed can fall
from a height of 30 metres, and that gives the descending
seed every chance of catching a lateral breeze and moving
a serious distance away from the parent tree. We had a
sycamore tree in the garden of my boyhood: sometimes in
spring before the lawnmower had come out of hibernation, it
would seem that we had gone for the revolutionary concept
of a sycamore lawn: hundreds of sycamore seedlings poking
their optimistic heads above the sluggish April grass, having
made a short but decisive journey by helicopter from the tree
that let them go.

Plants evolved in the water; their life on land is a comparatively recent development. But, as we have already seen,
the epic directionless opportunism of evolution has seen
a good few land plants subsequently evolve for the watery
life. This has given them different challenges when it comes
to distributing their seeds, so join me in my canoe on the
River Waveney that flows between Suffolk and Norfolk: in
some places and in the right season you can paddle through

a wild floating garden of flowers, mostly yellow water lilies. They grow in water and their seeds need to find water or they won't survive, so naturally they use water to spread them. If these seeds were to sink, they would be in direct competition with the parent plant. If they were to float, they wouldn't be able to germinate and find nutrients: they need to reach the bottom. So they do both: when the seeds are released they float but after a while they get heavy, lose their buoyancy and sink.

Mangroves, the small tropical trees that often line estuaries and coasts, take this a step further: the seeds germinate while still attached to the parent plant. They then drop like darts, at low tide sticking into the mud, at high tide floating upright like fishermen's floats, to be carried off to meet their destiny, if all goes well a vacant piece of coastal mud.

Some watery species place an each-way bet. When I paddle my local river on a still day in summer, it seems to be a solid floor, one that needs a good sweep: dust and fluff covers it. The fluff is in the air and all over the river: the seeds of willows, trees that love to have their feet in water and often line the courses of rivers. I paddle on through the fluff of willow seeds, and all of them are looking for the right place to become willow trees. At first I thought all the seeds in the water were losers, doomed to drown, all chance of germination gone, but that's not necessarily so. They can stay afloat for several weeks without rotting, to be hooshed gently downstream, or pushed back upstream with the tide, and the winners in the lottery will find a nice piece of soft bank where they can germinate.

Alders are also wet-loving trees, often found in small clumps called carrs on a riverbank. Their seeds are equipped with small wings, which enable them to make use of the wind. But trees that like to live along rivers must expect many seeds to find the water below, and alders are quite prepared for this eventuality. The seeds have pockets of air and two cork appendages, so they float well. They also resist the water very efficiently: they are still viable after a full year in the water.

There is, I suppose, a certain passivity in this, but so much of a plant's life is about waiting for something to happen to it. Plants can do a great deal to make desired events come about, events like pollination and dispersal, but by their nature there's not usually a great deal they can do all by themselves. However, one of the joyous things about natural history is that every time you think you have some kind of pattern established in your mind, you come across something that totally contradicts your assumptions.

Ivy-leaved toadflax is a plant of rocky places, and it carefully plants its own seeds. The stalk that bears the flower – and ultimately the fruit – at first grows towards the light, in the accepted manner of plants (phototropic, to be technical). But once the flower has been fertilised, the plant goes into reverse. The stem, bearing the fruit that carries the seed, now seeks only to avoid the light. The stem dives towards crevices and cracks in the rock wall where, if all goes well, the seed will find conditions suitable for growth. So the plant moves with purpose to plant its own potential offspring.

Some plants get rid of their seeds by firing them across the landscape as if from a gun. This doesn't sound very plant-like, but it's what happens with many deeply familiar plants, most notably gorse. You find gorse on open heaths and cliff-tops: bright yellow flowers, a million prickles and a rich figgy smell. Rather surprisingly, they are legumes and so related to peas, and like peas they produce their seeds in a pod. These slowly dry out, and they do so unevenly in sunny weather, the sunny side drying faster than the shaded side. This inequality sets up tensions in the pod which make it split open with some violence, squeezing out the seeds as a bar of soap squeezes from your hand in the shower. On a good day they achieve a reasonable distance: 5 or 6 metres, enough to have a chance of germinating away from the parent. They explode with an audible crack: if you sit still for a while on a sunny summer afternoon in gorse country, you will hear a series of no-longer-mysterious snaps and pops.

Many plants use this strategy: the squirting cucumber is one of the more spectacular, firing seeds out in a fierce jet; other examples include lupins, geraniums (like the doves-foot cranesbill we met earlier) and a plant cheerily named touch-me-not: if you do touch it, you might release the seeds. Perhaps the champion at ballistic dispersal is the sandbox tree of the Americas, also known as the dynamite tree: scientific name *Hura crepitans*. It can release seeds at a speed that's been calculated at 160 mph, for distances that have been claimed at more than 100 yards. More conservative estimates make the average distance closer to 30 yards – still a seriously impressive effort.

Gorse likes an each-way bet. The seeds that it forces out with such vigour are coated in a rich mixture of fat, protein and sugars. These are of great interest to certain species of red ant, which will carry these seeds further, so that the great gift of nutrients can be enjoyed; a similar strategy to the primrose met earlier in these pages. Often the ants use these seeds to feed the larvae back in the nest. The ants are only interested in the coating, so the seed itself is safe. The seed covering is there as a bribe – just reward if you prefer – for the ants' part in dispersing the seeds. So there they are, conveniently underground and awaiting the moment to germinate. The ants haven't just dispersed the seeds, they have planted them as well.

Animals are better than plants when it comes to movement, so many plants get animals to move their seeds about. Broadly speaking, there are two ways of doing this: by moving seeds on the outside of an animal and by moving them on the inside.

A plant gets an animal to move seeds externally by sticking the seeds to the animal. The burdock is a master at this: the burs it produces can be a bugger to get rid of. The burdock plant is familiar to many of us, and there are some on the Entangled Bank: big flabby leaves that are distinctive even before the plant – it's a biennial – has put up its flowering spike in its second year. The flowers are pleasing, a bit like thistles, which are relatives; the roots are edible, favoured by foragers, and part of mainstream cuisine in China and Japan. They are also used to make the ancient drink dandelion and burdock. The seedheads take the form of little prickly balls, excellent for use as missiles in children's games, matting the manes of hairy ponies and ringing the socks of walkers. They stick to the fur of dogs and wild mammals; there have been reports of birds getting so thoroughly burred they can no longer move.

A Swiss inventor named George de Mestral took a walk with his dog, Milka, in the Alps in 1941 and both of them brought a good few burs home with them. Their effectiveness intrigued him, so, being that sort of man, he tried to find out how they work. He admired the stickiness of his burs and their reluctance to part company with their perambulating hosts, so he examined them under a microscope and found that they work on a system of tiny hooks mating with tiny loops. It was a eureka moment: he invented Velcro.

Mistletoe mostly employs birds. The plant is a parasite that grows high in trees, its sticky seeds hold onto the legs of birds – and the birds tend to remove them when they are perched on another tree, often beak-wiping them onto a branch. The seeds can then stick to the tree, and high in a tree is precisely the place where mistletoe makes its living. More on mistletoe and other parasites in Chapter 22.

The outside method of using animals to disperse seeds is comparatively unusual. Many more use the inside method, which is rather less fancy: get eaten, stay viable, pass through the animal and come out somewhere else. We have already looked at blackberries: foxes and other animals binge on blackberries but the tiny seeds go straight through unharmed. And that's the secret of it: to find a way of passing through the gut of an animal – usually mammal or bird – without taking harm.

I once watched a bear in the mountains of Slovakia. It was feasting on berries: they can, it's been claimed, eat 400 in a single mouthful. And the seeds go through them pretty fast: a bear can distribute 20,000 of them across a square kilometre in an hour. We all know what bears do in the woods and the results of this are neither modest nor discreet. In this way bears create and maintain precisely the habitat that suits them best: sowing, fertilising and harvesting. Or perhaps the berries are exploiting the bears to their own advantage:

it's one of those circles of mutualism that give the human observer so much satisfaction.

Bears are thin on the ground in Britain these days; the last ones lived here about 1,500 years ago, and back then they most certainly did their fair share of seed distribution. But there are still wild birds and mammals to spread seeds about the place, and plenty of plants that rely on them. You can often make them out from their advertising: the bright red of rosehips and hawthorn berries – hips and haws – signal their edibility, and the nutritious wrapping is worth consuming, meanwhile the seeds mostly pass through undigested.

Seeds are nutritious in themselves but are usually well protected. The plant often wants the seeds to be eaten, but it's no help if they get chewed up or pecked to bits. (Pigeons carry grit in their crops, this helps them to crush the seeds they eat, which is bad news for the plant.) Finches have powerful beaks and can get through the outer casing to the seeds beneath, and that's no good to the plant either. But on the whole birds are a better bet than mammals: they have no teeth so they will often swallow the seeds whole, and they have wings, so they can take the seeds further.

Oaks rely heavily on jays and squirrels to transport their seeds. But their seeds are big and well protected in a shell. No bird or small mammal is going to swallow an acorn whole, still less pass it out again intact. Both species consume them by breaking the acorn open and eating the nutritious kernel: squirrels mince them with their ever-sharp rodent teeth while jays chisel them to bits with their powerful beaks; neither ploy is, at first sight, very helpful to the parent plant. Jays and squirrels rely on acorns to get through the winter and there's no point in leaving them on the tree and coming back later: they will fall off, and besides, some other creatures will get them if you don't. So both species hide them. I have often seen grey squirrels burying acorns from my window as I write.

In autumn jays are very visible – you usually hear them before you see them – a great screech like a length of cloth being ripped, magnified a thousand times. They take three or four acorns at once, apparently swallowing them whole – but they are just being stored in the gullet for easy transport. There's generally one more for luck in the bird's beak.

The jay then conceals them in a series of hiding places, generally holes in the ground. They have an extraordinarily precise memory for these caches, but they are unlikely to get to all of them in the course of a winter, not least because they might die before it's over. It's been estimated that a jay can cache 3,000 acorns in a single autumn – and a good few of them will escape being eaten and germinate. But even then, they are not, so to speak, out of the woods. Jays are no fools; they are reckoned to be equal with great apes when it comes to intelligence, as we humans understand the term. When they see an oak seedling, they know there is an acorn underneath, and that a bill is as good for digging as it is for chiselling.

It sounds as if the jays have the edge in this relationship, but if that was true they would eat out their own food supply and both species would suffer and perhaps go extinct. This doesn't happen because oak trees will in some years produce a synchronised overproduction: what's called a mast year, when all the oak trees in the area produce a superabundance of acorns. It's a strategy called predator satiation: there aren't enough jays and squirrels to eat them all. They will bury as many of them as they can, but there are so many that they will never eat them all. If they did this every year there would, all things being equal, be more jays and squirrels around to eat them. But the superabundance always takes the two populations by surprise: there are never enough predators, and so the strategy works.

I know all this sounds rather chancy. An acorn needs to be harvested for food by an animal that doesn't get around to eating it, and it must be cached in a suitable place for its germination and growth. After that it must hope to survive its delicate early years unmunched by deer or domestic mammals (or intelligent jays), and also to survive competition from other plants, sometimes of the same species, for resources like water, nutrients and sunlight. All these things must go right before an acorn can become a full-grown tree producing viable acorns of its own. The odds against a single acorn becoming a mature oak tree are colossal. Even in a wild state without competing humans, you might put the odds at about a million to one.

In a mast year a single oak can produce about 10,000 acorns. In the tree's natural span – well beyond the century – an oak tree can produce a million acorns. And it only requires one acorn to become a mature oak tree for the parent tree to fulfil its biological destiny and become an ancestor. In this way, what looks like a long shot becomes something more like a stone-cold certainty.

Sycamore Gap
before
2023

11

BRANCH MANAGER

Is not Love a Hercules
Still climbing trees in the Hesperides?

Shakespeare, *Love's Labours Lost*

Four or five years of my boyhood were spent on an intense botanical study. My subject was the plants of Streatham Common, and the work was of a depth, an intensity and an intimacy that few botanists ever achieve. True, I couldn't name the species of many if not most of the subjects of this extended investigation, but that was because the concept of species seemed irrelevant. I knew them far better than most people who knew the difference between oak and ash. I knew them as individuals.

Streatham Common is divided into two by a road called Streatham Common South. The westerly side is a mown sward with a few trees here and there. The eastern chunk has a formal garden called The Rookery and 30 acres of woodland. Trees. It was a world to be explored with stealth and daring: a place of adventure.

I knew some trees better than the rest: of those I knew best, I understood each one as a tree unlike any other in the world. I studied them with all the senses, most particularly that of touch. It was not a study that led to a conclusion; rather it was a dynamic relationship, or a series of dynamic relationships that took place all over the wood.

I climbed them. John Murtagh lived three doors away; we were both nine or ten when we started, a great age that meant that we were trusted to cross Streatham Common North unaided. Of course we played football and cricket on the open parts of the common, each according to season as was then the way, but more often than not we went into the woods. And climbed.

We climbed easy trees and we climbed difficult trees. I liked the way that some trees opened themselves up to the climber, obligingly throwing out branches at just the right points, so that we could get up them as easily as climbing the stairs, sometimes to poke our heads beyond the foliage and survey the canopy of leaves that led in one direction to Norwood Grove and in the other, back down The Rookery. There was a pleasure in the rhythm of these undemanding climbs, the familiarity and the certainty of the handholds that became footholds, the trustworthiness of the branches, even those high off the ground.

The difficult trees offered different things. There was naturally the pleasure in conquering them, in getting one-up on the tree. There was also the sense of admiration and respect for those trees that couldn't be climbed beyond a certain point, or couldn't be climbed at all. It wasn't supposed to be easy: we weren't supposed to win every time, only to try.

We had different skills. John was taller and stronger, with greater reach; I was more agile. He was better at the bottom, when getting into the tree at all was a challenge; I was better at the top, when the gaps between branches were narrower and the branches themselves more slender.

The basic manoeuvre of tree climbing is something we called the Sloth. It's often the move that starts a climb: grasping the lowest branch above your head, facing the trunk and smearing your plimsolled feet up the bark until they are higher than your head and your hands. At this point you hook your ankle and then your knee over the branch you are hanging from, and then comes the key moment: a sort of squirming heave that ends up with you sitting astride the branch with your back to the trunk. Then you can grasp the branch above you, stand and turn inwards to the trunk: looking upwards for the next branch that will take a foot.

There was a thrilling reek of double jeopardy in all this. The first was the park keepers, men in brown suits and brown trilbies (each one bearing its brass badge) who did what they could to stop us, not because we might hurt ourselves but because of the damage we might do to their charges: their concern was the health and safety of the trees. The second was the inevitable dangers of climbing. Naturally we had our falls: skinned knees from accidental slithers, skinned hands from losing grip, occasionally lumps and bruises from tumbles. I remember one fall from quite a height: a vivid kinaesthetic memory of reaching out a hand as I fell backwards, feeling the bite of a branch against my palm and fingers. I failed to hold on but the botched grab straightened me out:

I landed on my feet rather than my back, rolling at once as I did so in an instinctive and inelegant break-fall. I was good at falling, though it's not a skill to be proud of: the better climber doesn't fall. And then – undoubtedly – we went on to the next tree and climbed.

John and I didn't compete with each other. Climbing was a purer thing than that: it wasn't about us, it was about trees. I was an adroit and rather showy-offy climber in the gym at school but that wasn't the same thing at all: on Streatham Common it was about being in the woods, with no one to see, climbing living trees, dodging the parkies, performing the Sloth high above the ground, moving delicately upwards by way of the slender untrustworthy branches at the top – the closer to the trunk your feet, the safer you were – finally reaching the canopy, looking out at the meadow of leaves and the sky above and then at the leaf-covered acorn-strewn ground so far beneath your plimsolls.

I have already mentioned the sycamore tree in the garden. It wasn't a bad height; when you climbed it your head was on the same level as the roof of the house, or a little higher. It wasn't a hard climb because the branches grew at sympathetic intervals, but it took a little nerve, because once you were above the bedroom windows they got thin and whippy. I climbed it often, not so much as a challenge as a celebration of intimacy. One day a neighbour from lower down the road spied on me and confronted me at school the next day: why had I climbed the same tree half a dozen times in succession? I knew even then that in some matters, if people need an explanation they'll never understand.

It's about trees.

Cuckoo pint

12

THE ENTANGLED BANK, PART 3

Where, like a pillow on a bed,
A pregnant bank swelled up, to rest
The violet's reclining head ...

John Donne, 'The Ecstasy'

It was early July: time to walk the Entangled Bank once again. The lane had had only three weeks to recover from its mowing and I wasn't convinced there'd be much there. Fleeting views from the car window gave the impression that it was all green, very few flowers at all and the bracken growing even stronger than the nettles. There was, however, one flower I was confident of finding and the first lot – a great crowd of them – was right by our forever-open gate.

1. Hedge bindweed

Lord, these are lovely things, when viewed with an unprejudiced eye: a wall of trumpets, pink and white with arrow-shaped leaves making beautiful the most unpromising places. A chain-link fence in a junkyard will, given an ounce or two of neglect, become a thing of beauty and joy at least until the end of the summer. Hedge bindweed will climb up trees and hedges and anything else, using long grasping tendrils that seek for a grip. You can see them from train windows in season: banks and fences and bramble-brakes dripping with the stuff.

But bindweed has an equivocal reputation. It is immensely skilled at taking over: given a free run over a season or so, it will turn a small shed into a flowery tent. That's all very well for the passing stranger, but it creates problems for those who wish to make the decisions about what grows where.

Bindweed is good at getting its own way. It has a massive and complex root system: 9 metres deep is no problem, and growth three times deeper has been claimed. The plant can sprout from seeds twenty years old, and it can regenerate effortlessly from pieces of severed root. Gardeners and allotment holders wage war on the plant, and many will resort to chemical herbicides. Turn your back and bindweed will destroy the place by means of its beauty.

2. Cuckoo pint or lords-and-ladies

Sorry. I really should have noticed this one before. Somehow I missed the flowering season of this wonderful plant, one already familiar to me. Perhaps I was unlucky with the timing, but more likely I was unlucky with the skill-set I possess. I may be better than I was last year, but if I missed this little wonder in flower, there's clearly scope for improvement. Still, at least I found two or three examples of the plant bearing the berries that the flower produces to disperse its seeds (poisonous to mammals, but not to birds). You find them as a little knob of berries close to the ground, bright red in a few weeks but now a modest green.

The flower is subtle but not modest. You don't need a particularly dirty mind to see this as a plant with both phallic and yonic implications: a chunky purple spike enveloped in a cloak of flowing green; I have an ambition to produce a metal sculpture of this flower, say, 10 metres high on the Thames Embankment. It will be a masterpiece, one that celebrates sex in the nicest possible way.

The common names reflect the plant's inescapably sexy associations: cuckoo pint, rhyming with bint rather than a pint of beer, can be traced back to an archaic term for penis; lords-and-ladies might be better spelt with apostrophes. There are many others: the fanciest is Kitty-come-down-the-lane-jump-up-and-kiss-me; a more recent version is willy lily.

3. Knapweed

Here is a handsome plant that looks like a thistle and is related to thistles, but doesn't scratch. There was only one in the lane; you're more likely to find them in dense stands on grasslands, where they have a tendency to dominate an area. The flowerhead is a purple shaving-brush, though it can also be pink and occasionally white; the leaves are longish, thin and pointed. It comes from a genus of around 700 species. It's a good, rich nectar source and favoured by many species of insects; it's a particular favourite of common blues.

4. Common ragwort

This is not so much a plant as a controversy. It's a native British species but there have been serious campaigns to drive it to extinction, despite being one of the most important nectar sources around, used by a good 200 species of insects, and is the sole food source for thirty of them. The most frequent user is the cinnabar moth; in adult form this is a daylight flier, a lovely thing of crimson and bottle-green; the black-and-yellow caterpillars feed on the leaves of ragwort.

It's a tall, straggly plant with a cluster of twenty or so yellow flowerheads, daisy-like in shape. The leaves look feathery. The plant grows on abandoned ground and road-sides, but it's most often found in paddocks and pastures. It grows well in such places because, unless desperate and not necessarily even then, grazing mammals won't touch it: it smells bad and tastes worse. The poet John Clare wrote admiringly: 'thou waste of stinking blossoms'. It's also highly poisonous.

This is a powerful and effective defence mechanism, but it doesn't work once the plant is cut and served up in hay (dried grasses) or silage (fermented grasses). These are two important foods for keeping horses and cattle going at times when there's no good grazing available (like winter) but they are potentially lethal if you allow ragwort to get in. The plant becomes palatable in hay and silage, but retains its toxicity.

It can cause cirrhosis of the liver. I have heard harrowing tales about its effect on a horse's brain: the horse's eye functions normally, but the messages no longer reach the brain, making the animal functionally blind. It's listed as one of five 'injurious weeds' in the 1959 Weeds Act (which means injurious to agriculture, i.e., profitability). It is subject of the Ragwort Control Act of 2003, which establishes a code of practice but no legal obligation to get rid of it. That would be impossible: the stuff is common, tough, disperses well and grows readily.

Here is another example of how plants impact on human lives. 'He paints the wayside flower,' says the hymn, but this flower, which I duly found on the wayside, is not universally considered bright and beautiful. In Ancient Greece the plant was believed to have aphrodisiacal properties. They made a concoction from the plant called satyrion, from its association with lustful satyrs. It is mentioned, perhaps inevitably, in Petronius's masterpiece *Satyricon*.

5. Field bindweed

The flowers are smaller than those of the more common hedge bindweed, but they're still trumpets, or perhaps cornets. Most of the flowers I found were white, but one small clump was striped pink and white, as if the result of generations of careful nurture to please human eyes. This is more a creeper than a climber – one of its nicknames is Creeping Jenny – though it can climb a few feet in favourable circumstances. Despite its delicate beauty, it is, like hedge bindweed, a tenacious plant much disliked by gardeners.

6. Thistle

Perhaps I should have put this in Chapter 2, as one of those flowers that everyone knows: tall, with spiky leaves and a love of growing in great clumps, and a purple pompom on the top. There was one on the Entangled Bank: as uncompromising a thistle as ever pricked the thighs of a passing human, splendid in its resilience, its sharp-edged weaponry against grazers honed to perfection.

There are many species of thistle; this was creeping thistle, the most common, a great enthusiast for untended places. It throws up shoots again and again from its vigorous, chunky rootstock, forming those dense colonies that are so much easier to walk around than through. The more elegant and robust spear thistle is (it's usually agreed) the origin of the Scottish emblem: tough, intransigent, perennially ready to defend itself. Other species of thistle include woolly, meadow, tuberous, dwarf, marsh, slender, Plymouth, musk, cotton and milk. Richard Mabey writes that thistles can be eaten: the young shoots, stripped of their spines, can make a salad while the hearts of the flowers are like 'miniature globe artichokes'.

7. Catsear

Also known as flatweed, and sometimes, like so many others, as false dandelion. The plant makes a low rosette, to dodge grazers and, by implication, lawnmowers, and throws up a central spike that forks and bears neat yellow flowerheads. The stem is solid, unlike the hollow dandelion. The leaves are softly fuzzed, which gives them their name.

8. Great hairy willowherb

There were just a few of these, which I found on the way back and near the house: tall stems, some of them reaching 6 feet, with pink flowers, each with four notched petals in a rising column at the top and a white spot in the middle. They like wet places: damp grassland, ditches, riverbanks. When I take my kayak on the local river in July, there are great stands of them, lush and confident. They are also called just great willowherb or hairy willowherb, the hairiness a reference to their downy stems.

They're related to the rosebay willowherb, which is common and widespread and routinely turns railway verges pink: one of those joyous sights that show what nature can do to delight us, when given half a chance. It's worth taking a moment to look at this plant, and odd to think that at the beginning of the twentieth century it was a scarce woodland species. It can be tall, 3 foot is easy, 6 is possible. The plant has long, pointy leaves (lanceolate) topped by magenta and pink flowerheads with no white spot, four petals with four pink sepals behind, so it's like two crosses.

They're known as fireweed in North America, because they tend to spring up after a forest fire, opportunists making a profit from the devastation. They spread in Britain after the First World War, when many forests were clear-felled, a process that mimics the effects of fire. But they're more closely associated with the war that followed: when the cities of Britain were bombed, the devastated areas were colonised by extravagant gatherings of rosebay willowherb, and the plant was nicknamed bombweed.

Though the plants imparted a sinister beauty to the shattered cities, they weren't regarded with any great romantic pleasure: life springing up in places of death and all that. Rather they made it uncompromisingly plain that the great cities were being bombed back into wilderness: the seas of magenta, adding such vividness in the high summers of the Blitz, were an unignorable reminder of how badly things were going. Now the plant is just another coloniser of broken and untended land: enough to turn your head briefly as you walk down a country lane or to raise your eyes from your phone as the train emerges from a tunnel.

So there, on a third walk along the Entangled Bank and just three weeks after the casual swipe of the mowing machine, were eight new species, showing once again that disaster for some is opportunity for others.

Oak

13

WHAT DO YOU MEAN, TREE?

The tree which moves some to tears of joy is in the eyes
of others only a green thing that stands in the way.

William Blake

Yes, indeed, Mr Blake, but what *is* a tree? This is a question
that seems to come from the realm of the bleeding obvious,
but in fact there's no precise definition – legal, botanical or
even commonsensical. You might suggest that if it's got wood
it's a tree, but that makes heather a tree, so it won't do. So you
can say that if it's a very tall plant it's a tree, which is true
enough, but you've missed out the ankle-high mature trees
you get on mountain tops and the tundra: dwarf willows, for
example. And you've also included some species of bamboo,
which can be grown for timber and reach 30 metres in height,
but bamboo is a kind of grass.

Tree is not a botanical category. As we've already seen, conifers are gymnosperms while most of the rest of the plants on this planet – including oak trees and rainforest giants – are angiosperms, and that's as far apart, in terms of evolutionary history, as a modern plant can get: as far apart as, say, beetles and mammals. The fact is that the strategy of rising above the rest – getting closer to the light and so getting more of this most valuable stuff for yourself – is so useful, and if you like so obvious, that it has evolved several times over. This is called a convergence, and you find convergent evolution again and again once you start looking: true flight evolved four times over by four quite separate evolutionary routes, with birds, with bats, with insects and with the extinct pterosaurs (the group that includes pterodactyls).

There is also the question of when is a tree not a tree? Are the elders on the Entangled Bank trees? Or are they shrubs? It's an informal bit of classification and is strictly a matter of taste. Science makes no distinction here. Lord Denning looked for a workable definition of a tree for the 1990 UK Town and Country Planning Act and came up with this: 'Anything that one would normally call a tree is a tree.' And if that lacks precision, it is at least something we can work with.

There are about 3,000 species of native trees on the island of Borneo: I have walked the rainforest paths near the Kinabatangan River, looked up at the canopy 100 metres above my head and marvelled. Britain and Ireland have about thirty-five native trees, including a few that some people would call shrubs. The reason the number is so low is because 18,000 years ago, an ice-sheet 3 miles thick covered Europe as far south as Berlin, and so no tree could grow.

As things began to warm up 10,000 years ago, life began to migrate back towards the North Pole. In Europe the process was held back by the east–west mountain ranges, the Alps and the Pyrenees, so Europe has half the native trees species of North America, where there is no such obstruction. And then, in a process that finished about 6,000 years ago, the seas rose again as the ice continued to melt, flooding Doggerland, the area of low-lying land that connected East Anglia with Holland and the continent of Europe, and no tree species could cross it. That has left Britain very low on native tree species.

But you will meet several trees beyond the native three dozen on most walks. That's because where the ice, the mountains and the sea stopped the march of the trees, humans have made up for it and planted exotic trees all over the place. It's been going on since the Romans came over in AD 43, and it's happened with many species of plant; trees are merely the most obvious. Plants established across the centuries are archaeophytes, or old plants; the more recent ones are new plants, that is to say, neophytes – so when you describe yourself to a good botanist as a neophyte, you are calling yourself a plant. When does an introduced plant become a neophyte? The cut-off date usually agreed on is 1494, the year of the first voyage of Columbus. After that date, plants from the New World began to be introduced all over Europe, many of which got out and went feral.

There are about 60,000 species of trees in the world, perhaps as many as 25 per cent of all living plant species. Most of them are angiosperms, sometimes referred to as hardwoods, though the hardness of the wood varies considerably from species to species. The life of all trees is usually based on a twin strategy: grow tall and live long, with the result that the tallest living things and the oldest living things on Earth tend to be trees. Examples: Hyperion, a Californian redwood tree in Redwood National Park, California, is 116 metres tall; Methuselah, a Great Basin bristlecone pine in the White Mountains in California is just shy of 5,000 years old. The tallest native tree in Britain is a beech in Newtimber Woods in Sussex, which stands at a comparatively modest 44 metres; the oldest is probably the Fortingall Yew in Perthshire, between 2,000 and 3,000 years old, though local patriots will give you an argument about that.

Trees have a trunk, sometimes more than one, that lifts the leaves above other competing plants – or at least, that's the idea. The leaves are the light-gathering devices, the food-making devices, the power-generating devices that drive the tree and allow it to grow tall and live long. It follows that the more leaves a tree has, the more powerful it is. This is in line with one of the great differences between us animals and them plants. The rough basic principle is that animals are maximal inside, while plants are maximal outside. A tree dramatises that principle better than any other living thing.

Trees are made from wood, as everyone knows. Wood is made from cellulose fibres forming tubes that are strengthened with lignin, a complex organic polymer: a polymer is a substance made from very large molecules. This strengthening allows the tree to be self-supporting, to grow tall and in short, to be a tree. The living wood is protected by bark, which comprises dead cells of phloem, or cork. It provides a waterproof overcoat, protecting the living inner tissue from easy consumption, fire and hard weather. Trees need an extensive root system, one that not only brings up water and nutrients from the soil but also keeps the tree anchored in stormy weather.

Plants need water; if you don't water your house plants, they die. Liquids travel through vascular plants by way of dedicated vessels, which are analogous to the vascular systems that we vertebrates all possess, i.e., veins and arteries. But trees and other plants don't possess a beating heart to pump liquids around their – sometimes vast – bodies: they must do the job without muscles to do the hard work. The method they use is one of those bafflingly elegant things that pull you up short again and again. It is worth being a bad botanist if only to marvel at the way a rainforest giant and your nearest oak tree get water from the ground up into the canopy. Xylem cells are formed and as soon as they're formed, they die. But their cell walls maintain their strength, and these form extremely narrow tubes – just a few microns wide. (A micron is one millionth of a metre.) These tubes connect the roots (which gather water) to the leaves. Leaves have small holes in them (stomata) and, from these holes, water in the tree evaporates. This creates negative air pressure in the leaf – and that pulls up water through the vascular system of the tree. It only takes a small difference in air pressure to bring this about because the vessels are so narrow: imagine sucking on a drinking straw. It's easy to get your drink – it would be much harder if you were sucking a drainpipe. That beautifully simple method gives life-giving movement of liquids to a static giant. It operates alongside the phloem cells that carry nutrients created by photosynthesis down through the plant to the roots. Xylem and phloem operate in all vascular plants, most spectacularly in the tallest trees.

And while you might think that you can't tell one kind of

tree from another, and may even have claimed as much in conversation in order to stress your bad botanical credentials, I'm prepared to bet that you can name a good half-dozen. As with flowers, you know more than you think. Let's put that to the test.

1. Oak

The oak – at least, the oak species we're all familiar with – has unmistakable wavy-edged leaves and in autumn it carries equally unmistakable acorns. Oaks tend to look like oaks even to the botanically unawakened, and are often obvious enough even in leafless winter: strong and uncompromising, wrinkled bark, often standing alone in a stretch of parkland or on the boundaries of a field.

There are several species of oak found in the UK and about 600 worldwide. The one we call the English oak (*Quercus robur*) is the national tree of many other countries, including France and Germany. Oakwood has been used to frame houses and to make ships; the warships this country produced were called the wooden walls of old England.

2. Horse chestnut

Horse chestnut trees are a quintessential part of English life, standing on village greens and parks, offering a generous shade and easily recognised at every stage of their growing year. Strange to think that the plant wasn't introduced into this country until the beginning of the seventeenth century.

People brought it in because they liked it: it was often used to adorn parkland owned by wealthy people. (It's become a rare species in the world, and is classified as Vulnerable.)

In spring their sticky buds are celebrated and used for early indoor decorations in vases. The wide fingered (palmate) leaves are unlike anything else, and the flowers – sometimes called candlesticks, a good analogy – are wonderfully dramatic. In autumn they produce fruit containing the chestnuts, more usually known as conkers, because of the traditional game in which one nut conquers another.

3. Conifer

There are many species of conifer to be found in the UK, most of them introduced, but if you can tell a conifer from other kinds of tree (normally referred to in this context as broad-leaved trees), you are making a botanical distinction. We refer to many of them with almost equal lack of precision as pine trees.

A good few species of exotic pines have been brought into the country for commercial plantations, faster growing than the native Scots pine. We recognise conifers from their needles, the way they bear cones (pine cones or fir cones) and because they (mostly) don't shed their leaves in winter. That last trait has thrilled us for centuries and still does: that's why we bring them into our homes at the darkest time of the year to celebrate the fact that with these still-green trees, life visibly continues. So we decorate them with lights and call them Christmas trees.

4. Silver birch

The silver birch is easy to tell from the rest because it's silver. Or to be more accurate, very pale indeed – the bark is almost white, broken up by darker fissures as the tree gets older. It's not in any way a dominating tree, like an oak: the leaves are small and comparatively few, it gives a dappled shade, allowing plenty of light through, creating a microhabitat for mosses and other things to grow beneath it.

Silver birches can cope with a wide range of temperatures and are pretty tolerant all round. They are also, for a tree, fast-growing, and that makes them highly suitable as pioneer trees. When a patch of ground is left to its own devices, it's likely that the first tree to colonise the place will be a silver birch. This is part of the ecological succession and we'll take a closer look at this in the next chapter.

5. Weeping willow

Willow trees are natives and well loved by those that can recognise them, but the weeping willow, stretching down to the water in loving fronds, is a neophyte, native to North China, where it has been cultivated for centuries. There's a story that the first weeping willow in England was cultivated by the eighteenth-century poet Alexander Pope at his riverside home in Twickenham, and that all other English weeping willows are its descendants. That's not actually true, but these generous, water-loving trees are now as much a part of English life as the horse chestnut.

6. Flowering cherry

In spring the suburbs and parks of Britain burst into pink froth and that's mostly because of Japanese flowering cherry trees. They are descended from trees that were cultivated in Japan, from two different species, neither of which bears fruit that's palatable to humans.

There is something rather splendid about this, despite all the stuff about the importance of native species: here are trees, a substantial investment in space and time, cultivated on a vast scale simply for their beauty, one that can only be perused for a couple of weeks a year, shorter if there's a storm. The flowering cherry is probably the most widely cultivated ornamental tree in Britain, though they don't naturalise. But since it's another tree you can recognise without difficulty, it's entitled to be on this list.

7. Apple

These fruit trees give a gentler kind of blossom than the intense Japanese cherries, and what's more they have edible fruit at the end of it, which is why most of us can pick them out from the rest. Crab apple trees are wild and native and bear small bitter fruit: the crab apple is one of the ancestors of the cultivated apple, of which there are more than 6,000 cultivars.

Apples are particularly associated with the United States and apple pie is part of the American identity. But apples were put to another, perhaps more important use in the pioneering days: they very easily turn to alcohol and this can very easily be distilled into applejack in the freezing continental winters – just leave it outside, scrape the ice off occasionally and drink up. That's what helped the pioneers to get through the winter, but it gave them powerful hangovers – this rough-and-ready method of distilling doesn't remove all the impurities.

8. Holly

We'll all know holly, an essential part of Christmas: holly leaves on the plum pudding, holly wreaths on the door knocker so that every caller can be benignly pricked. This is another evergreen, brought into our homes to reassure us that life will return and the winter will pass. The blood-red berries give another layer of vividness to the plant.

The annual veneration of holly predates Christianity but, like so many other ancient traditions, it was seamlessly adopted. On grey winter days in apparently lifeless stretches of woodland, the holly, with its lustrous green leaves and glowing berries, is as inspiring a symbol of life as you can find on a winter morning.

Water lily

14

WHY YOUR GARDEN IS NOT AN OAKWOOD

Change and decay in all around I see . . .

From the hymn 'Abide with Me' by Henry Francis Lyte

Perhaps you're a gardener. What are you doing when you're weeding a flowerbed? Perhaps you think you are tidying up, removing the weeds, what the French so charmingly call *mauvaises herbes*, naughty herbs. What you're actually doing is stopping your garden becoming an oakwood. Should you mow a lawn, you are not just controlling the length of grass and knocking the heads off daisies and dandelions and pre-empting any possible infestation of doves foot cranesbills. You are also making sure that grass remains the dominant plant of the stretch you have mowed. You are stopping it from becoming an oakwood. When the local authority runs a tractor with mowing blades around your local park, they too are part of the anti-oakwood movement. When arable farmers harvest, plough the field and sow wheat seeds, and likewise when dairy farmers turn out cattle to pasture, they are, yes, preventing the fields and pastures from becoming oakwoods.

I remember vividly the moment when I first grasped this essential point: when I understood what is meant by the ecological succession. I had always vaguely believed (without ever once actually thinking about it) that an area of open grass existed because it was grass, and that this was an immutable state. An area of heathland was the same because it was, well, heathland, while an area of marsh and for that matter, an oakwood itself, were destined to carry on forever – as they were today, so they would be forever.

I was introduced to a startlingly different concept when I was at the great RSPB nature reserve, Minsmere. The then-warden Jeremy Sorensen was trying to explain to me how the place worked: to get me to understand that Minsmere is as much a managed landscape as a field of oilseed rape or Kew Gardens or your local park or your window box. 'That reedbed,' he told me, 'is doing all it can to become an oakwood. We are doing all we can to keep it as a reedbed, because if it stops being a reedbed we won't get marsh harriers and bitterns and bearded tits breeding here anymore.' So the RSPB is continually removing brambles and shrubs and scrub and willow, because if they didn't, the reedbed would stop being a reedbed.

Every ecosystem – any patch of land, any patch of water – is dynamic, not static. It's there as it is, at any one moment, because stuff is happening, and the place is continually changing because stuff continues to happen: seeds germinate, plants grow, plants are eaten, plants die. In many places we humans have taken control of the process of change: you can manage a patch of bare earth and flowering plants in order to keep it as what we call a flowerbed, or you can leave it unmanaged and it will take its own course. But stuff is happening all the time in every ecosystem on Earth, even if you keep restoring it to the state you wish to impose by mowing and weeding and other forms of management.

It's a simple principle; it's an extremely complex process with uncountable variations. It was first described by Georges-Louis Leclerc, Comte de Buffon, generally referred to as Buffon, the great eighteenth-century scientific pioneer, and one of the great names of the Enlightenment. It was originally studied mostly by botanists. The process was seen as a succession of different kinds of vegetation because that's exactly what it looks like. But it comes about because of the interactions of all forms of life: plants, animals, fungi, bacteria – everything that lives is part of the process of life, and it is moving, shifting, living, dying, forever in flux.

A patch of open freshwater won't be there forever as a nice big pond – not if it's left to its own devices, not if it's left to the actions and interactions of nature, not if the ecological succession is given a free run. This pond is changing even as you look. The water may be too deep for rooted plants, but it supports floating organisms and freshwater plankton. As sediment is deposited by natural processes, from the water systems that feed it, from the effect of rain on the banks, from the general effects of movement, the water gets shallower and richer, and rooted plants like water lilies are now able to make a living. From there the process continues – it never stops – and you start to get plants that emerge from the water like reeds and flag irises; what you have is now a swamp.

The process of drying and thickening continues as the swamp becomes a marsh, with rooted plants growing on land, on *terra* relatively *firma*. Among these plants will be the seedlings of trees, brought here by the wind and in the droppings of birds and other animals. The wet-loving trees will be successful at first: willows and alders will eventually form clumps of mature trees known as carrs. But if left, these places will dry out still further and become less suitable for willows – and far more suitable for oaks. And when the oaks start to grow, they will continue to dry out the land, taking the water for themselves, and, if allowed to do so, will create a closed canopy woodland: the climax vegetation. All it takes is an absence of interference and a few centuries.

A closed canopy forest is as stable an ecosystem as you can get, but it's stable in the manner of a bicycle. A bicycle is only stable when it's in motion, and a forest is as dynamic an ecosystem as the open water it all began with. It's not going to change substantially in the normal way of things, but it's going to change in minor ways and will keep doing so all the time: it's a living system and life changes all the time. Let's take an exotic example: one of the great trees of the Amazon rainforest falls. As James Goldsmith famously said about marrying your mistress, this creates a vacancy. For the first time in a century or more, there is direct sunlight on this particular patch of forest floor. And the forest floor is a seedbank: seeds deposited decades back are still viable and they will respond to the sudden access to light and rainfall and germinate. The first to do so will be the relatively ephemeral plants: one spectacular example is the hotlips plant, which, when in flower, looks like a caricature pair of kissable lips: a dramatic message to pollinators to come down and act quick, for the window, the time in the light, will not last forever.

Plants like hotlips are sprinters; the great trees are marathon runners, who see time in a quite different way. And this leaves a gap – a vacancy – for the middle-distance runners, and a classic example of this is balsa, a plant with ultra-lightweight wood traditionally popular with the makers of model aeroplanes. Balsa is a forest tree that operates with devastating speed, though this is speed as a tree understands the term, rather than a cheetah. A year-old balsa can stand 10 metres tall, while a more orthodox tree will only be a few centimetres. The balsa draws up water and contains a great deal of loosely packed fibres reaching up to the canopy at a good 30 metres or more, and it then sets about the business of reproduction in just as much of a hurry, putting out great white flowers that are, rather surprisingly, pollinated by the little mammals called kinkajous. The plant isn't built for long-term survival and one that has reached its thirtieth birthday has done exceptionally well. These frail things are able to become ancestors, but not to be ancient trees: down they come, and often alongside a sapling has been growing well, exploiting the temporary shelter of the balsa, and is now ready for its own bid to join the canopy.

The same sort of process is going on in every flowerbed. If you neglect the weeding for a couple of weeks in the growing season, small ephemeral plants will start to grow, their seeds arriving in the usual way. They will germinate fast, flower as soon as they can and produce seeds very rap-idly: they can go through a lifetime in a few weeks, while oak trees think in terms of centuries. Leave this flowerbed for longer and more robust plants – plants that take longer to establish themselves – will move in. These are plants that play a longer game. Bees and other flying insects will move the pollen about, many animal species will eat the plants, and so the system moves on. Abandoned gardens in ruined houses tend to be dominated by brambles, which have taken a couple of years to establish a presence. These don't cover the ground completely, and yet they protect it from many plant-eaters, especially grazing and browsing mam-mals. That means they can act as inadvertent tree guards, keeping safe the seedlings of pioneer trees like silver birch – or more often, in many parts of lowland Britain, the exotic (neophyte) buddleia bush, so beloved of butterflies. And so the succession continues.

It was thought that at one stage, most of lowland Britain was a closed canopy oak forest, but this can't be the case because there was until recent years a hefty population of large wild mammals. The wolves would not have survived without substantial numbers of herbivores (another principle of ecology is that the numbers of prey animals control the numbers of their predators). These herbivores were wild horses, several species of deer, and the now globally extinct auroch, ancestor of most domestic cattle.

These grazers helped to shape the landscape. You can see how at Knepp Castle in Sussex, where unprofitable farm-land has been left to do as it wishes, with the grazing done by native ponies, deer and English long-horned cattle, who play the part of aurochsen (a plural to savour). Trees grow up where they can, but open spaces are maintained for grazing by the grazers themselves: living lawnmowers.

Ecological succession is much studied. It is traditionally divided into two forms. The first is primary succession: what happens – the orderly procession of species – after total destruction, like landslide or a volcanic eruption. The second comes from the disruption of an existing community, like clear-felling a woodland. The first is largely predictable; the second depends on the circumstances that existed before the disturbance.

Thus an ecosystem can move from exposed rock to lichens and mosses, to annual weeds to perennial weeds and grasses, to shrubs to pioneer trees to the climax. The classic example of this principle in action is the island of Surtsey, which lies off the coast of Iceland and didn't exist until 1964, when it reared out of the sea as a result of volcanic activity. It was declared a nature reserve the following year: only a few scientists are allowed to set foot there; this stops casual visitors inadvertently bringing seeds and other organic stuff onto the place. In 1965 the first vascular plant was found on the island; by 1967 mosses were visible; by 1970 lichens were present. Mosses and lichen covered the island, but the succession continued: in the next two decades twenty species of vascular plants were found there, of which ten became established. It was hard enough for any plant to make a living in the desperately poor soil, but the soil gradually got richer as seabirds started to use the island and dumped their droppings all over it. In 1998 the first bush was growing there, a species of willow. By 2008 the plant total had reached sixty-nine, of which thirty became established (there are 490 species on the Icelandic mainland). And the place continues to move forwards, with the plant total rising by two-and-a-half species every year. In centuries to come, some kind of climax vegetation will establish itself and this will have its own dynamic equilibrium – unless rising sea levels or volcanic activity change the circumstances once again.

Purple
loosestrife

15

THE ENTANGLED RIVERBANK

He thought his happiness was complete when, as he meandered aimlessly along, suddenly he stood by the edge of a full-fed river.

Mole, in *The Wind in the Willows* by Kenneth Grahame

A heatwave and a drought followed my last walk along the Entangled Bank, turning the grass to the colour of lager. Record temperatures were set, with a frightening high of 40.3 Celsius, five degrees higher than the peak of the famously hot summer of 1976. The effects were visible all around, so when I made my next walk along the lane in early August, I had no expectations of plenty. Nettles and bracken dominated most of the banks; the brambles seemed untroubled, with some of the stems (floricanes) putting out pink blossom. There were a few stems of ragwort; the berries of cuckoo pint, now bright red, were easily visible. Even the cow parsley was struggling a little. I found a stem or two of knapweed and some reasonably strong-looking catsear. All in all, it wasn't too bad for a drought: the shady conditions beneath the strong hedges probably helped. And rather to my surprise, I found two plants in flower that I hadn't recorded before.

1. Mugwort

This is an easy plant to overlook, but it's rich in traditional meaning. It's tall – a good metre – with deeply cut leaves: glossy above and greyish below. Tiny flowers line the top of the stems and look rather silvery. There is an interesting smell, said by some to be like camphor; certainly it is fresh, bitter, pungent and rather pleasing in a quiet way.

The plant has been gathered for medicine, food and drink. It was used to flavour beer before hops became standard. Roman soldiers put the leaves in their sandals to soothe their feet on long marches (a forced march in sandals doesn't sound much fun). Since then travellers have put leaves in their shoes to combat weariness. Mugwort has been used to help digestion and improve the circulation. A very similar mugwort species is found in China, Japan and Korea and it's used for moxibustion. You burn the dried plant on the human body in clumps called moxa, placing them on the pressure points (the points used for acupuncture and shiatsu). The patient puts up with this until it becomes uncomfortable, speaks the word and the highly localised blaze is extinguished. (I had the treatment once on a damaged knee; without any miraculous success, alas.) The leaves are also useful for repelling insects, especially moths.

2. Black horehound

Here's another plant that doesn't exactly clamour for your attention, fitting neatly into roadside verges, looking a little nettle-like – it's another of those dead-nettles – with discreet pinky-purple flowers along the stems. It's more straggly than the dead-nettle species we met earlier, the long stems sometimes curving, arching and falling away; the toothed leaves turn black later in the year. It has another, more vivid name: stinking Roger. It's been used medically for a number of ailments, including gout and depression.

This plant was not in an attractive state when I found it: it had flowered, with small pinky-purple, rather hooded flowers. The leaves, toothed and hairy as you would expect, were turning black. I had learned that the smell becomes a great deal worse when you crush the leaves in your fingers: research is never wasted, so I tried it out and my fingers stank merrily even after a prolonged scrubbing with a soap that offered a competitive scent. It's an effective defence against grazing animals.

So that was that: not, it has to be said, a terribly wonderful haul of plants, so let's leave the parched banks of the lane and turn to a place where the effects of the drought were less obvious. Let's go to my local river: a small and unpretentious river in the Broads.

One of the great pleasures of becoming a wildlifer is that you're always aware of wildlife even when you're not actively seeking the stuff: part of your life, always there. I have spent a great deal of time birdwatching on horseback, from train windows and, more recently, from my kayak along this and other rivers in the Broads. After my Damascene conversion on Orford Ness, I have taken to botanising – badly – while propelling my noble craft along the water: now, instead of just seeing pretty colours, I am observing plants. I'm now on first-name terms with all the more obvious species that grow on the bank, and that has added layers of richness to every paddle. So let's look at a few of them, all seen during the same high summer drought.

1. Yellow water lily

You don't paddle the Broads for the thrills of white-water. The flow is mostly gentle, and in some inlets and on the inside of some bends, it slows almost to a stop. In such unchallenging places a plant can get its roots down to the bottom of the river and flower in the air above it – part of the ecological succession, as noted in the previous chapter. Water lily leaves lie flat on the surface, held up by their cunning pockets of air, while the flowers rise on rigid stalks and hold themselves clear of the surface. The plants can easily cope with water 3 metres deep.

Water lilies are highly significant to both science and art. They help to explain – or least exemplify – the rise of the flowering plants, or angiosperms; we will look at the evolution of plants in Chapter 18. Water lilies were the favourite subject of Claude Monet: he painted about 250 water lily studies; there are eight vast canvases of water lilies, totalling 100 metres in length, at the Musée de l'Orangerie in Paris.

2. Purple loosestrife

The best place to be a flower during a drought is on a river-bank: here in these well-watered places, purple loosestrife gave an improbably lush air to the desiccated countryside. These are big, bold things that stand a metre and more in height, and in season (June to August) they carry a huge spike of reddy-purple flowers – you'd struggle to find a garden with such spectacular blooms. They rise in dense crowds, many spikes rising from a single rootstock. They are great nectar sources for long-tongued insects including the pale-yellow brimstone butterfly, red-tailed bumblebee and the elephant hawk moth, an insect as extravagant as the flowers.

The name is a bit of a puzzler. That brilliant but never wholly reliable Pliny the Elder says the flowers are named for the former king of Thrace, Lysimachus; the name from the Greek meaning 'lose strife'. It's also been claimed that placing stumps of the plant on quarrelling oxen will have them the best of friends again, having lost their strife.

3. Hemp agrimony

Here's a plant related neither to hemp nor to agrimony, though it looks a bit like both. I know, it's enough to make a bad botanist despair. Never mind, they're awfully pretty – and standing on a riverbank in company with the purple loosestrife, they are as stunning a pairing of flowers as you'll find anywhere in the world.

They have a clustery, cloudy head of many flowers, mostly of pale dusty pink, or raspberries with too much cream. They're perennials, often standing more than a metre, and they seem to stay in flower all summer, great favourites of butterflies. Butterflies, flowers – does nature get any more benign than this? It's as if it was intended entirely to please the eyes of passing walkers and paddlers: an oasis of life of the most pleasing kind in the long desert of summer drought.

The leaves do look a little like those of cannabis (hemp) plants; the scientific name is *Eupatorium cannabinum*. Richard Mabey (*Flora Britannica*) reports that the headquarters of what was then the Sussex Trust for Nature Conservation was once raided by the police who arrived (without a search warrant) to seize the plant, having been tipped off by someone who read the label without grasping its meaning.

4. Water mint

Sometimes when walking the marshes of Norfolk, I tread on these plants by accident and fill the air with mint. Here at last is a name you can trust: this plant really is a mint that likes watery places. On the bank of the river it was rising with toothed oval leaves, just as you would expect from any sort of mint, mauve flowers rising in little pompoms. Here's another perennial, another long-term flower that attracts pollinators. If that makes you suspect that these banks must be full of pollinating insects, especially butterflies, you'd be dead right. You can gather the leaves to make mint sauce or mint tea, or to put them in your Pimm's.

5. Flag iris

Or yellow iris or just flag. I always get rather fed up when ID books tell you that some plant or other is 'unmistakable'. I reckon that where plants are concerned, I could mistake anything for almost anything else. *It may be unmistakable to you*, I want to say, *but it ain't unmistakable to me.*

However, you'd have a job to mistake a flag for anything else when it is in flower: a huge yellow bloom that looks as if it had been cultivated for a garden. They're more common on the marshland that lies along the river floodplain than in the river itself, but you can find them where the flow is at its most sluggish and the river at its most shallow. These are emergents (so a significant plant in the ecological succession) and they grow in dykes and pools; the maximum depth they can take is about 30 centimetres. They stand tall, almost a metre, on chunky stems, flying a yellow flag that's huge and filled with nectar.

6. Meadowsweet

This is a wet-loving member of the rose family, and to a bad botanist at least, it looks nothing like a rose. Never mind, it's a lovely plant, standing up to a metre and putting out a great welter of frothing and creaming white flowers. It has a complicated scent, and a walk over the marshes in summer fills your nostrils with it, competing with the water mint. It's called meadowsweet because it was used to flavour mead, the fermented drink made from honey that gave so much solace to our ancestors; it's also been known as queen or pride or lady of the meadow.

7. Fleabane

Here's a damp-loving plant crowned with a collection of little suns: the flowerheads are broad discs surrounded by rays. The petals (all right, ray florets) and the disc florets in the centre come in contrasting shades, a dark orange middle surrounded by yellow rays. They like ditches and wet places and the riverbank suits them well, setting off the purple loosestrife and hemp agrimony, so that the overall effect is startlingly lush. Who planted them? Whose eyes were they made to please? Not ours: they are there for the compound eyes of insects, but our own delight in them won't do them much harm.

They have wrinkled green leaves which, when rubbed, give an odd smell that's described as a mixture of chrysanthemum and carbolic. They were used to repel fleas: hung in dried bunches or burned as a fumigant. This was probably reasonably effective; they are related to the pyrethrum plant, which is used for making mosquito coils; when burned they are extremely effective in chasing off mosquitoes.

8. Arrowhead

One of the great joys of getting on first-name terms with the common plants is that you start to notice the slightly less common ones. And in two or three places along my usual paddle, I was able to pick out a small emergent with flowers that glow a mauve so pale it's almost pure white, with a deeper purple in the middle, while the leaves are long and pointed, arrow-shaped. Finding and naming this plant was one of those unexpected moments of pleasure: a realisation that I am a slightly less bad botanist than I was a year earlier.

9. Himalayan balsam

Here is one of the classic conundrums of wildlife con-servation: how can something so beautiful be so bad? Himalayan balsam grows in great stands, sometimes almost 3 metres tall, with lush clusters of pinky flowers, usually described as shaped like a bonnet or a policeman's helmet. They have been nicknamed poor-man's-orchid and kiss-me-on-the-mountain.

They were introduced into this country in 1839 and within ten years they had got out, often with active help from enthusiasts who thought their beauty improved the rural countryside. There's a great bank of them on the townward stretch of my local paddle and I welcome them as I pass as beautiful but dangerous, like Nicole Kidman in *Paddington* or Faye Dunaway in *Bonnie and Clyde* or – this being an Asian plant – Michelle Yeoh in *Crouching Tiger, Hidden Dragon*. The plant has reddish stems, pointed (lanceolate) leaves and when the flowers have gone, it bears long green seedpods that explode and send their seeds up to 4 metres away.

They are good because they are lovely, and bad because they grow with immense vigour and crowd out native species. Wildlife organisations try to get rid of the stuff, traditionally with balsam-bashing parties. Some fear that this approach only prepares the ground for another invasive plant, Japanese knotweed. There are experiments in using rust fungus for biological control.

The problem of invasive species can't be solved on a good-guy-bad-guy basis ... and there's only one sure solution to unwanted exotic species: don't bring 'em in.

wheat

16

TAKING CONTROL

God said unto them, 'Be fruitful, and multiply, and
replenish the earth, and subdue it . . .'

Genesis 1:28

Wild carrots have already come up in these pages a few
times; you can find them in the British countryside looking
nothing like carrots as most of us understand the term: that is
to say, a tapered orange root. They are lofty umbellifers, and
if pulled, the root doesn't seem to be worth eating, or even
edible. I have also mentioned the wild roses that grow along
the Entangled Bank: they don't look much like the roses that
you give or receive in a loving bouquet. These are the wild
originals – or something close to them. The carrot on the
plate and the rose in the vase are the results of domestication.

This is a concept that every botanist – and for that matter,
every zoologist – must get to grips with. The difference
between wild and domestic plants is not that one grows all

by itself and wherever it likes, while the other grows where and when a human tells it. It goes much deeper: humans have taken the plant – and changed it. A wild carrot and a wild rose are no more like the familiar domestic carrots and roses than a wolf is like the Labrador sneaking onto the sofa – and yet all domestic dogs are descended from wolves. A plant or an animal (or for that matter a fungus) becomes domesticated when humans take charge not of behaviour but breeding.

A good few animal species have been domesticated, for food, transport, rodent control, protection and companionship: three dozen or more. The number of domesticated plants is uncountable. One estimate reckons that fourteen large mammals have been domesticated for agriculture – and 2,000 plants. And we have domesticated plants for many more uses than food: as flavourings, medicines, intoxicants, perfumes, hallucinogens, for oil, fuel, fodder, cooking oil, textiles and enrichment of the soil – plus a good few thousand simply because their beauty pleases us.

It is very hard to domesticate an animal. Animals need food and water, they often need to be cleaned up after, they often need to be confined and perhaps most importantly, they bite or gore or kick, and what's more, they run away. Animals move, which is highly inconvenient of them. They are hard to keep alive; any farmer will tell you that from birth every sheep has one single ambition, which is to die. The domestic animals we have today are the result of long programmes of selective breeding designed to minimise all the above inconveniences and to maximise all the things most useful about the animal in question. If you were a primordial farmer trying to tame a herd of wild cattle – the now extinct aurochsen – you would make sure only the nice docile ones did the breeding, while the fierce and intractable ones were killed and eaten as soon as possible. That way, and not even by design, you would end up with a herd of progressively more biddable animals. It takes skill, it takes commitment, it takes nerve and, above all, it takes time.

But you can domesticate a plant yourself, today, this very minute. All you have to do is find a few wild plants of the same species, take them home, and try to keep them alive, at least until they produce seeds. The next step is to grow more of them from these seeds – always choosing seeds from the plants you like best, for their size or their colour or their edibility. Once you've taken control of the breeding you have, in a rough-and-ready fashion, a domesticated plant.

The domestication of plants was the second great leap forward for humankind. The first was control of fire, which was also made possible by plants: the process of making fire from a platform of softish wood and a spindle of hard wood gave humans control of fire about a million years ago. Agriculture was invented about 12,000 years ago. It happened in several different places in the world at the same time, quite independently. It was just in the logic of human development, and also, perhaps the result of a fall in global temperatures that made food harder to find and so made hunting and gathering a less certain way of life.

Wheat was first cultivated in the Fertile Crescent, which is a hugely significant place for the European civilisations that followed. This is an area of land along the Nile and between the Tigris and the Euphrates, the three great rivers of antiquity, and it was one of the key places in which humans ceased to be wanderers and became settlers: in which humans swapped a leisurely if often uncertain lifestyle for one of greater certainties and ceaseless labour – at least for some. It was a new life and it allowed humans to increase in numbers and to move across the planet.

This new life was possible because humans not only grew their own plants: they modified them. The wild ancestors of the wheat we cultivate today are not nearly as obliging as the modern plants. The seeds are what we want from wheat, so that we can grind them, mix them with water to make flat and leavened breads as well as porridge. But the wild species don't obligingly present their seeds ready for harvesting as the modern domesticated strains of wheat do. Wild emmer wheat, one of the ancestral plants to the one that many of us consume most days, is a kind of grass. The seedheads are a lot hairier than those of most varieties of domestic wheat. These bristles are called awns, and I trust that the triple-letter square in your hearts lights up at such a word. The seed uses the awns in order to plant itself. When it's ripe, the seedhead at the top of the plant's stem shatters and the seeds fall to the ground. With the increased humidity of the night the awns grow stiff and draw together, but they relax again the following morning as they dry out – only to change again the following night. This sequence of dry-wet-dry allows the seed not only to move but to propel itself into the soil. You might expect this system to make the seed oscillate on the spot, advancing with the wet and falling back again with the dry, but the seed carries tiny hairs that grip, allowing it to maintain its advanced position: it carries on moving forward when the night and the dew return.

This is a great adaptation for a wild plant but a bad thing for humans wanting to consume the seeds. But selective

breeding has done away with that trait: with modern varieties of wheat the seeds stay obligingly on the plant, waiting
for harvest-time – first for a scythe and now for a combine
harvester.

Wild plants have all kinds of disobliging adaptations.
Many of them have a nasty taste, developed specifically to
discourage potential eaters. After all, a plant's gameplan is
not to get eaten and usually – in the wild at least – it's the
species that don't get eaten that survive and become ancestors. Wild pea plants have exploding seedpods like gorse.
It's a hard thing if your nice crop of peas scatters its edible
parts all over the landscape: an ancestral pea can shoot them
a good 4 metres from base.

Some plants are tasty enough but not suitable for domestication, being resistant and inconvenient. Most of these no
longer play much part in our lives; one of the few wild food
plants regularly exploited by humans on a large scale is the
tree that provides Brazil nuts. They don't do well in plantations and have to be gathered wild in rainforests. Another
problem with wild plants is that many are equipped with
factors that sometimes slow down the rate of germination:
some will sprout later than the rest. This is a useful trait in
cold places: sometimes those that germinate early will be
killed by a spring frost. This favours the late starters, while
in warmer years, the early plants will have a head start and
do better. Variable times of germination is a strategy that
allows plant species to cover their bets. Again, this is a sound
policy for a wild species, but not helpful to a farmer who
wants all the plants to grow at the same rate so they can all
be harvested at the same time.

There is a further important factor. Plants tend to vary, and variation is hugely important. Changing conditions will suit some of these variations more than others. Variation gives robustness to any species; variable germination times is just one example. But variation is hell when you're farming: a farmer wants each seed to breed true to its parent and each one of these to be as near as dammit identical. That's what makes farming viable.

Over centuries humans took control of the breeding of their domesticated plants (and animals), which ceased to be wild. Modern wheat is not viable as a wild plant – how can it be? It can't drop its seeds to earth to sprout. It can never, under its own steam, become an ancestor.

Annual plants are the most suitable for domestication, along with some biennial or perennial plants that can be treated as annuals: you take seeds from them every year and every year plant a new crop. With an annual you can select a new generation every year: that means you can change the plant far more quickly than you could with, say, an oak, which takes several decades to produce viable seeds. You select and plant the seeds that come from parent plants which have the most useful traits.

Domestication and selective breeding allows plants to become suitable for environments other than the ones they evolved in: wheat, a plant from West Asia, is now grown all over the world. We select for the ability to resist disease, for the ability to function as an annual, for the loss of seed dormancy, for the inability to scatter seeds, sometimes for less efficient breeding and even sterility, for sweetness, for lack of toxicity, for the large size of the edible parts and for the ease with which the edible parts can be separated from the rest of the plant.

All those decisions across all those years have created the many plants we grow on a large scale: plants we find on supermarket shelves, fresh, dried, tinned, packeted, frozen, pickled, processed or turned into bread, biscuits, cakes and pasta. They are plants that humans have changed, that humans devour, that humans exploit. But you can look at it from the plant's point of view. The ancestral grasses that gave us wheat would have stayed as localised plants, one among many, just like the wild grass species we find away from cultivation in this country: species like foxtail and Yorkshire fog. But, unlike Yorkshire fog, wheat has conquered the world. It has done so because it entered into a strange and complex relationship with humans. It couldn't have done it on its own – but it's probable that humans couldn't have got where they are today without wheat. Wheat covers endless uncountable acres, an expanse of the globe that would have seemed quite ludicrous for an insignificant wild grass 12,000 years earlier.

You can argue, then, that wheat has exploited humans, and by doing so has become one of the planet's dominant plants. Or you could see this as mutualism: a symbiosis in which both parties benefit. As the oxpecker helps both the giraffe and itself by feeding on the giraffe's external parasites, so humans have helped both wheat and themselves – or wheat has helped both itself and us, if you prefer.

Humans have looked after wheat, have kept endless acres of land safe for wheat, have killed the plants that compete with wheat, have killed all the invertebrates that might eat the wheat, have killed all the fungi that might benefit from the wheat, have planted the seeds of wheat and treated the land with nitrates that benefit the wheat. The list of losers is a long one, but humans and wheat are winners on the most massive scale.

And as humans have selectively bred many thousands of plants for their usefulness, so we have also bred many others for their beauty. This was, inevitably, a later development than the domestication of food plants: it couldn't be done without food security and leisure, and it probably couldn't have been done without a leisured elite.

We mostly think of a rose as a flower with a tight head of twenty or thirty tightly clasped petals that make a complicated cup. There are varieties with huge numbers of petals, up to 200 (technically these are multiple flowerheads rather than single flowers). But as we have seen, a wild rose is a much simpler thing. It has just five petals and opens right up, so as to be available to pollinators. The huge and the very tight cultivated roses are unable to admit pollinators: they have been bred to please humans, not to enhance the sexual lives of roses, or for that matter, the welfare of bees. That means they can only be propagated by cutting and grafting: in other words cloning, by producing genetically identical versions of themselves, or by hybridising with other cultivated species. They can't exist – in the sense of passing on their own genes and becoming ancestors – without the help of a gardener. Among many other things, cultivated roses, especially red roses, have become symbols of sexual desire:

> *O my Luve's like a red red rose*
> *That's newly sprung in June . . .*

But they can't have sex themselves.

So when we look at wildflowers – what most of us think

of as basic botany – we are looking at organisms that have got there on their own, while many if not most of the plants that you see in a well-tended garden will be domestic varieties that have been bred from wild ancestors, and are often radically unlike them.

Roses were originally cultivated for their fragrance, which can be transferred to humans, covering up bodily odours or otherwise increasing the charms of the scented person. The easiest way to do this is to make rose water: just simmer the petals in water. But soon enough roses were also cultivated for the beauty of their appearance; they were associated with the excesses of the Roman Empire. (It's said that Cleopatra seduced Mark Antony in a bedchamber covered in rose petals.) Roses have been bred into forms and colours impossibly remote from those on the Entangled Bank: climbers, ramblers, shrubs, miniatures, hybrid tea, polyanthus, floribunda, grandiflora – and on and on. A nice rose garden is a collaboration between humans and nature: a halfway house in which nature is welcome and cherished, but only on human terms.

Domesticated plants often get out and go wild, for some are still capable of breeding on their own; Himalayan balsam, already mentioned, is a classic example. Roadside verges in the arable countryside often have free-growing brassica (cabbage) species that have come from farmed varieties; the daffodils on the Entangled Bank aren't the traditional English Lent lily in pale yellow, but a cultivated variety with bright orange trumpets.

Botany is the study of plants, and that's a much bigger subject than I had bargained for when I first contemplated those wonderful plants on the shingle of Orford Ness. There's a botany lesson on every shelf in the store cupboards and fridges and bread bins of our houses, as well as in the gardens that occur in every human living space, however densely populated. The history of the modern world – from the last 12,000 years – is the story of a radically altered relationship between humans and plants. First they made us: now we have made them.

Beech

17

MORE TREES

Fond lovers, cruel as their flame,
Cut in these trees their mistress' name;
Little, alas, they know or heed
How far these beauties hers exceed!

Andrew Marvell, 'The Garden'

This chapter is about the trees that you think you should know already but are too embarrassed to ask: the slightly less obvious trees, the trees other people seem to know without even trying. We'll keep off the conifers for a moment – here are seven species of what are called broadleaf trees, even if their leaves aren't necessarily all that broad: the angiosperms. Some of these trees are natives: they've been with us since not long after the last glaciation 14,000 years ago. Some grow wild. Many have been planted by humans in the belief that they will do us good: to provide food for humans, fodder for domestic animals (often as wooded pasture), for timber and fuel and to mark boundaries. They have also been planted because they look nice, because they are good for our souls, because trees capture carbon and absorb pollutants and give out oxygen and water, because trees are important in many forms of nature conservation and because most places look better for a tree.

Half a century back, there was a campaign to 'Plant a tree in '73' – it was founded on the romantic notion that any tree anywhere is an improvement. That led to some odd anomalies: I once saw a grazing marsh in Suffolk planted with, among other random species, a Japanese flowering cherry. Here the trees were drying out the soil and stopping the marsh from being a marsh (see Chapter 14 on the ecological succession), which was hard luck if you happened to be a marsh-living species like ducks and geese and southern marsh orchids and flags.

This is not, in any sense of the term, to come out as anti-tree: it's to make the point that some planting is better than others. Remember that almost all the landscape of Britain has been shaped and managed by humans over the centuries; usually a tree is growing because humans have either planted it or tolerated it.

1. Beech

Beeches make people go soppy. They're associated with femininity, a sweet contrast to all the butch, uncompromising oaks; I suspect that's because oaks have deeply wrinkled bark where the bark of beeches is smooth. Beech bark is a shade of grey that looks silver in the right light and when seen by the right eyes. Favourite trees are referred to as queens.

Woodland beeches make a dense canopy and little grows underneath: your feet stir up leaf litter and crunch on the shells of nuts, beechmast. The leaves are oval and pointed, with prominent veins that make a V either side of the central stalk. They were late arrivals, reaching Britain under their own power just a few thousand years ago, before the sea rose up again, and they colonised in the south between the Bristol Channel and the Wash. They have been much planted elsewhere: in woodlands, in small copses, in avenues and as singletons in parkland.

They are often pollarded, which can give them a rather chunky appearance. Humans not only plant trees where we feel they're needed, we also shape trees to suit our own needs and fancies. Many trees are pollarded: that is to say, their heads are cut off – as a result, they branch out from the point of the cut, rather than rising in a straight trunk. We also coppice trees: that is to say, cut them down close to the ground. If you choose the right tree to coppice, a series of new slender trunks will arise from what's left, which is a coppice stool. The resulting poles are useful for all kinds of purposes, as we will see in a moment.

2. Willow

I mean the aptly named crack willow here: a tree of riversides and flood-prone country, one that grows fast and frequently splits, cracks and drops branches under its own weight, with a little help from the wind. If you think of a weeping willow as all downward, try to imagine it all upward and you have a crack willow: the same thin, pointed leaves, with the tree reaching up in stiff, whippy twigs.

If you allow the fallen branches to stay where they dropped – or to drift downriver until they find land – chances are they will put down new roots and start up all over again, clone of the parent. My wife (the practical one) once made a bird table from a willow branch: it was soon a small tree with a feeding station attached.

Willows grow naturally along rivers and are often planted there on purpose to stabilise the banks. They are frequently pollarded, which cuts down the opportunities for cracking. The pliable wands that sprout from the cut are used for weaving, though for serious basket-makers the related osier is the tree of choice.

Since willows like wet places, Edward Stone, an eighteenth-century parson, wandering about while suffering from ague or fever – probably a rotten cold – reasoned that they must have been put there as a cure, since fevers are also associated with damp spots. He nibbled the bark and it actually worked: he got better. What he found was later synthesised and marketed as aspirin.

3. Hawthorn

A hawthorn can reach 15 metres, so it qualifies as a modest tree, but it's more often found as a chunky bush, more often still as part of a hedge. It's also called May tree because it blossoms in May: the old advice – ne'er cast a clout till May is out – doesn't mean wait till the end of May, it means wait until the May tree blossoms.

The blossoming hedgerow is a trap for bad botanists: it's not just the hawthorns that blossom so sweetly. Wild plum and blackthorn flower a good deal earlier, and do so even before their leaves appear. Hawthorn trees do their stuff later, when the trees and bushes and hedges froth with white blossom – or sometimes with pink. There's an ecstatic passage in Proust's *À la recherche du temps perdu*, in which the narrator is enraptured by hawthorns – and then finds a still greater rapture with a pink one. 'Taking its place in the hedge, but as different from the rest as a young girl in holiday attire among a crowd of dowdy women in everyday clothes ...'

The flowers give way to bright red berries, which are much sought after by winter thrushes and waxwings. The leaves are deeply indented – lobed – and the twigs, of course, have spines. They grow thick and impregnable, naturally as spinneys, or with human direction, as hedges, a process radically speeded up when the fields were enclosed in the eighteenth and nineteenth centuries; it's reckoned that 220,000 miles of hedges were planted in that time – and an awful lot of that was hawthorn. Hawthorns are part of natural and social history.

4. Hazel

Hazel just about qualifies as a tree; if it's left alone it can rise up to 12 metres and live for eighty years. But it's a favourite tree for coppicing, and if the process is carried out regularly, a hazel can live for several centuries. If you see a coppiced tree – that is to say, a stump with many stems growing from it – chances are it's a hazel.

That's not, obviously, diagnostic, so a bad botanist learns to look a little closer, and the smooth, shiny bark is another good clue. The leaves are round, just about heart-shaped,

with a toothed edge, a pointed tip and a feel of gentle hairiness; the leaf feels pleasingly soft in the hand. In autumn
and winter the plant bears – no big surprise here – hazel-
nuts, which protrude from a leafy husk. In spring the plant
is full of lambs' tails, the male catkins, and if you look
properly, you will, of course, always see the tiny red female
flowers as well.

The poles that grow from the coppice stools have the
virtue of growing pretty damn straight, and they have been
used for many different purposes, including tool handles
and woven fences. They were also used for building: you
make a lattice of hazel wands and then pack it with clay
and animal dung. It's called wattle and daub. I once lived
in a Tudor house that suffered some damage to the walls;
repair work revealed the ancient building materials: sticks
and cow shit.

In managed woodland, coppiced hazels were grown
alongside oaks, which was the standard Tudor building
kit: oaks for the skeleton, wattle and daub for the flesh. The
method of planting, coppice with standards, is pleasingly
ordered to the human eye and surprisingly good for wildlife, and for that reason some woods are still managed in
this way. Dormice like hazel coppices and in the south of
England, nightingales nest in the heart of coppice, from
which they fill the woods with inviolable voice.

5. London plane

If you identify any street tree in London as a London plane,
the chances are you'll be right: more than half of them are.

And in most other cities in England as well. They've been planted in temperate cities all over the world: North and South America, South Africa and Australia. You want a street tree: plant a London plane.

They're probably hybrids between the American and the oriental plane, though that's disputed. Certainly they're full of hybrid vigour. They're tough, very seldom drop branches, can cope with any amount of pruning – London planes are often pollarded – have no problem when the base is paved over, and their roots can operate effectively in compacted soil full of rubble and rubbish. Better still, London planes can deal with pollution: there are London trees more than two centuries old; they have survived the industrial revolution, the years of pea-soupers, leaded petrol fumes and the various continuing pollutions of today. Sooty deposits and dust particles tend to wash off the shiny, rather leathery leaves.

London planes were introduced into Britain in the seventeenth century and extensively planted in the nineteenth. The leaves are large and hand-shaped (palmate) with five lobes and in autumn they produce round, spiky green fruit. Their resilience has been a blessing to city-dwellers across the years and the globe.

6. Ash

The more words I write in this book, the more I am tempted to pose a fount of plant wisdom – but I find myself brought up short when typing the word 'ash'. There is a particularly lovely ash about 20 yards from my desk as I hit the keys – when we moved into the place ten years ago, I didn't know what kind of tree it was.

Well, I know now. It stands a good 35 metres tall, pollarded a good many years back and so dividing at 12 feet into three stout trunklets or extra-stout branches. Ash leaves are quite distinctive: each one comprising several pairs of leaflets – up to a dozen of them – with a single terminal leaflet to round things off. The bark is grey and smooth. Ash trees flower before they leaf, unobtrusive things mostly insect-pollinated at night, which helps to explain why our place is good for both moths and bats: moths feed from the flowers and bats feed on the moths. The leaves fall while they're still green; the seeds hang in bunches called keys, because that's what they look like, and they're a favourite food for bullfinches, who nest in the garden.

Ashes grow swiftly and are not traditionally well regarded, having neither the toughness of oaks nor the elegance of beeches. They sprout enthusiastically from seed, and some foresters are inclined to regard them as weed trees, despising them as 'volunteers', but they have a certain resilience to biffs and bangs and that makes them useful for sporting equipment: billiard cues, oars and hockey sticks. For the same reason they also make the best walking sticks; in *Ulysses*, Stephen Dedalus carries one. 'He took the hilt of his ashplant, lunging with it softly, dallying still.' In Rudyard Kipling's school stories collected as *Stalky & Co.*, the prefects are allowed to carry 'a ground ash', for walking with and for beating bad boys.

A few years back the fungal disease chalara was accidentally introduced into Britain. It causes die-back in ashes and is now widespread, almost ubiquitous. It hasn't yet found its way to the tree in the garden, something I give thanks for on a daily basis.

7. Sycamore

The sycamore is widely regarded as the ultimate weed tree, and it's certainly very good at growing and propagating itself – which is, after all, a tree's job. They were introduced into Britain from Central Europe around 500 years ago and have never been much liked. They have large palmate leaves; on younger trees these grow on distinctive red stalks. The flowers are yellow-green and comparatively subtle; the seeds have wings and perform gratifyingly as helicopters when thrown in the air, as we did in the school playground. The sycamore in our garden in Streatham remains a special thing in my memory.

These seeds travel well and sprout avidly, which means they have populated roadsides and railway embankments. The leaves then fall on the line where they make a greasy paste that causes the wheels to slip: sycamores are largely to blame for autumnal train delays caused by 'leaves on the line'; they are, alas, the wrong sort of leaves.

We tend to dislike any species, plant or animal, that flour- ishes in environments which humans are trying to control: sycamores, nettles and rats all fall into that category. In woodland, sycamores crowd out native species of trees and shade out native woodland plants, but they have their good points. They may not support a great biodiversity of inverte- brates, but they do support a hefty biomass, notably aphids. What they lose in variety they make up for in numbers, and the invertebrates they support feed many bird species. Sycamore wood is pale and attractive, popular with turners, and often used in kitchens because it's nice to work with and it shows the dirt.

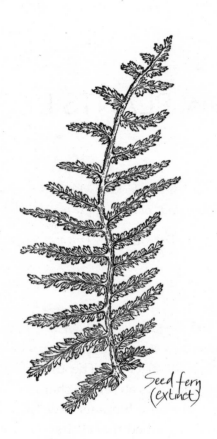

Seed fern
(extinct)

18

HOW PLANTS BEGAN

Can the principle of selection, which we have seen is so potent in the hands of man, apply to nature?

Charles Darwin, *On the Origin of Species by Means of Natural Selection*

Charles Darwin began *The Origin of Species* by not discussing natural selection. Instead, he talked about what he called 'artificial selection'. The first chapter, 'Variation Under Domestication', is about the changes in different species that take place once humans have taken control of the breeding. Darwin studied this at first hand by becoming a pigeon-fancier: he noted how vastly different-looking pigeon varieties – tumblers and pouters and fantails – all spring from the same ancestral species: the rock dove *Columba livia*, which is also the ancestor of all the urban pigeons in the world. One species can give rise to many vastly different forms ... so let me remind you that all pet dogs are domesticated wolves. A wolf is *Canis lupus*; a Pekinese, a Great Dane, a Poodle and a Labrador all belong to the same subspecies of wolf: *Canis lupus familiaris*. Once humans take control of who breeds with whom, massive changes can take place in a remarkably short space of time.

Working on the principle that you're not going to improve on Darwin, I have already written in Chapter 16 about the way that domestic plants are now very different from their wild ancestors, noting that wheat and roses are almost unrecognisable from the plants they sprang from over a timescale that can be measured in mere thousands of years, reaching a point when many of these cultivars can't even propagate themselves without human assistance. That's variation under domestication: artificial selection.

So now, still following Darwin's lead, let us move from artificial selection to natural selection, and the way it operates on plants over a timescale measured in millions. Time is the big thing to grasp when it comes to evolution, or rather, the fact that evolution operates on a timescale that we humans really can't grasp at all. Our minds, evolving for our own survival, work on the understanding that a year is quite a long time and a human lifetime is a very, very long time. We shake our heads in disbelief at the way humans lived a century ago, when motor cars were rare things, aeroplanes were wild exoticisms, flu was reliably lethal, contraception was unavailable and infant mortality was high. We can, if we make a huge effort, just about get our heads round the idea of agriculture beginning 12,000 years ago. But beyond that, forget it. Our minds just don't have the equipment for time in such quantity. We can sort of understand it intellectually, but we can't grasp it at all in any easy, intuitive sense. A

million years is no easier a concept than a journey to Proxima
Centauri, the nearest star; 600 million years ago, the amount
of time that has passed since the first algal ancestors of plants
appeared, is not the sort of time we are comfortable with.
We can only get there by thinking against the grain of our
own minds.

Darwin didn't invent the idea of evolution. Rather he
showed us how it worked, how it must work: by natural
selection. And when he explained this in 1859, people hated
it. They hated it because it destroyed our self-aggrandising
myth of human uniqueness. But if we weren't, after all, spe-
cially made in the image of God, how did we come to be?
Humans couldn't cope with the bleakness of Darwin's truths,
so we came up with a new myth: evolution is OK because it's
all about us. Evolution is a march of progress and it reaches
its point of perfection in humanity. This wonderfully con-
soling idea is expressed in one of the most significant bits
of iconography in Western civilisation: the famous sequence
of scuttling monkey, knuckle-walking ape, stooping early
hominid and upright perfect white Western male. The idea
caught on and remains mainstream because humankind
cannot bear very much reality.

And it's a wonderful idea all right – apart from the fact
that it's not how evolution works. Evolution has no goals,
it doesn't seek perfection, and it isn't even about ever-
increasing sophistication – indeed, as we'll see later, many
species lose complexity when complexity becomes counter-
productive. Evolution is about surviving and becoming an
ancestor: and, as T. S. Eliot wrote in a not dissimilar context,
that's all, that's all, that's all, that's all. And if you happen to
vary from the others around you in a way that favours your

ability to survive and produce viable young, you're more likely to become an ancestor than those that lack this variation. Those of your offspring that possess the same trait will in turn be more likely to become ancestors, and those that possess this trait in an even more favourable form will be even more favoured as ancestor material. They will, in short, be naturally selected.

And that's all fine and dandy until conditions change. Giraffes would find their long necks pretty silly if all the tall trees on the savannah dropped dead; water plants don't do too well when the pond dries up; the dinosaurs died out when a meteor hit the planet 66 million years ago and a certain other dominant life form is going to find its future compromised by alterations in climate that are of its own making.

Evolution does not have a plan, evolution is not about seeking perfection, evolution is not about improvement and evolution is not driven towards ever-greater complexity. Evolution does not create a hierarchy of higher and lower organisms: it produces individuals with ancestral potential. Evolution is not a ladder: it's a bush with millions of growing tips – each one equally valid – and what validates it is being alive. Now let's look at non-metaphorical plants.

And straight away we come to the problem of beginnings. Once again we must face the limitations of our own minds. We can grasp the nature of a tree or a daisy, and we can have some kind of intuitive understanding of a lion or a lamb. But coming to terms with microscopic blobs that may or may not count as living things is much harder. Some prefer to leave all beginnings to God, others to science, for once again we find ourselves thinking against the grain of our minds.

But let's try. It began with particles that developed the ability to use the energy of their sun for their own purposes. The earliest evidence for photosynthesis has been found in fossils 3,000 million years old. It was perhaps the single most decisive step in the development of life, and therefore, should the point need stressing, of ourselves – and it's a green blob far too small to see. Everything we have ever thought about the greatness of life comes down to that invisible green blob.

It started with a blob and it required years far beyond our easy understanding, even if we can add them up on a calculator: 3,000,000,000 years ago and a speck of green that was to make possible a world full of life. Then green algae with functioning photosynthesising cells joined up and found that cooperation gave them an edge, a favourable trait for survival and ancestry. They developed an ability to procreate by means of single-celled scraps of life that can develop into a larger organism: spores.

Plants developed in water but we humans are land chauvinists, and what we really want to know is how plants got to colonise the dry places of the earth. The answer, once again, is very, very slowly: perhaps at first on the edges of drying pools. The challenges were immense: drying out was death. Light brings life, but on dry land there was light in shattering superabundance, unfiltered by water. All the same, the potential rewards were high: those green spludges that managed to survive had the place to themselves. The land became populated by plants like liverworts.

But perhaps you are none the wiser. You don't often hear anyone exclaim: 'I say, look at this liverwort!' They are multicellular plants, but still pretty tiny: a few millimetres wide and a few centimetres long. They can make a living in all kinds of places, on stones and open ground. They're non-vascular: they don't have a system for passing liquids through themselves, and that puts a limit onto the overall size.

The development of a plumbing system was one of the great breakthroughs. It came about because of lignin, a substance that gives strength and rigidity to cell walls, and so allows plants to stand up for themselves. Lycophytes could reach a decent height but made their living without leaves, using scales instead. Hornworts had a waxy coat that stopped them from drying out easily. Such a coat would suffocate a plant, but it's punctured with small holes called stomata, and these make it possible for the plants to breathe, or to be accurate, to engage in the exchange of gases, taking in carbon dioxide and passing out oxygen – all plants except liverworts have them. This changed structure allowed plants to retain more water, and they were able to use this to create structure. Now plants could start to be tall. Some plants stand up because of the water they retain within themselves, which is why house plants droop when you forget to water them. But lignin can be stacked and interwoven in plants to become rigid, holding their shape under desiccation: so some plants became woody.

Club mosses developed leaves with veins and also roots. Roots anchor a plant and bring in water and nutrients, but they have their existence in the dark so they need the sugars – required for growth – to be brought down to them because they can't access light to power themselves directly. They are able to do so by means of a system for transporting sugars around the plant, called phloem.

Ferns developed complex leaves, though they still relied on spores for reproduction, and that made them dependent on the proximity of water. But a new group called seed ferns developed. They're now extinct; the name is only half helpful: they're not technically ferns at all. But they did have seeds, and that was a breakthrough. A seed, multicellular, capable of remaining dormant until conditions are right, and above all, not needing to be in water to germinate, was a game-changer. Plants could now move further and further away from open water. The vast spaces of land were opening up to plants – and therefore for all the other forms of life.

Gymnosperms produce naked seeds, and the group includes, as we have seen, all the modern conifers. And then came the next major development: plants that produce a flower with an ovary in which a seed or seeds can develop and be protected while doing so. These were the angio-sperms: the flowering plants. There are now around 300,000 known species of angiosperms and they make up 80 per cent of species of green plants. When we refer casually to plants – in a garden, or on an entangled bank – as flowers, we are not so very far wrong. We live in a world of flowering plants: flowers define our world.

There aren't enough fossils in the world for total certainty about the history of life. We have to look at it the other way: we're lucky to have the ones we've got. But the gaps in the fossil record troubled Darwin, who at a number of points in *Origin* said plaintively that the right sort of fossils – those that backed up his theory – really *would* be found sooner or later. He was right: Archaeopteryx, a creature indisputably transitional – a missing link if you prefer – between reptiles and modern birds, was discovered just two years after the publication of *Origin*. But the fact remains that the fossil record is still patchy, full of gaps and leading to all kinds of uncertainty. Darwin referred to the origin of angiosperms as 'an abominable mystery', and there is still no incontrovertible answer in existence now as to how they sprang up.

The earliest fossil angiosperms are 100 to 145 million years old, though finds of pollen suggest that the group may be a good deal older. No one can name the immediate ancestor of all angiosperms with any certainty. Perhaps the important thing to remember here is that while the purpose of science is to seek all the answers to absolutely everything, no one is claiming it's ever going to get there. Science is a continuing process of discovery rather than a parade of certainties: perhaps that's also the right way for us humans to conduct our lives.

The important thing to understand about the development of angiosperms is that it is a story of cooperation. Flowering plants were able to work so effectively because they recruited animals to help them. Animals made the great plant revolution possible, and that was greatly to the benefit of both parties.

Many species began to develop flowers that were decorative as well as functional: the decoration performed the function of attracting insects. Insects carried the pollen – male genetic material – from flower to flower, and the efficiency with which they did this allowed plants to form all kinds of outcrosses, which produced vigorous offspring. Outcrossing brings vitality to any gene pool: call that Lady Chatterley Syndrome – she preferred to mate with the gamekeeper rather than members of her own inbred class.

Of course, many angiosperm species are still wind-pollinated, which is imprecise, though as we have seen, it works well enough with grasses. But most of them work with animal species and that's because they evolved together: coevolution. Many flowers have both male and female reproductive organs. This is good, because in a single visit an insect can deposit pollen and collect pollen, two jobs in one, reducing the random nature of insect visitations. It's bad because in theory a plant could fertilise itself, which would bring an end to genetic diversity and outcross vigour. As a result, many flowering plants developed self-incompatibility: they are unable to accept their own pollen as fertilising material.

The angiosperms then developed bilaterally symmetrical flowers, a step on from the simple circles – radially symmetrical – that had been the norm for 70 million years. These more complicated flowers could invite specialised pollinators and greatly increase the efficiency of their sex lives and the reproductive process. We will look at the ways this operates in orchids in Chapter 24.

As flowering plants developed, so animals did the same thing. The forces of evolution produced warm-blooded creatures like birds and mammals: powerhouses of energy, creatures that move about a great deal and require a rich source of food or fuel in order to do so. These animals turned to plants for this purpose and in turn the plants took advantage of them. The angiosperms produced energy-rich seeds, often encased in tempting fruits, which were offered to the animals, who ate them and moved on, passing out the seeds in other places, often far from the plant that provided them.

Thus, flowering plants employed animals in order to have sex and to look after their progeny. The animals got energy in the forms of nectar, pollen, seeds and fruits. Who is exploiting whom? One more unanswerable question, but no matter which way you slice it, it's the way that the world hangs together.

Toadflax

19

THE WAYSIDE MONSTER

The clever men at Oxford
Know all that there is to be knowed;
But they none of them know half as much
As intelligent Mr Toad!

Kenneth Grahame, *The Wind in the Willows*

It's not usual to look for wildflowers in the middle of October, but I wouldn't like you, dear reader, to think of me as a skiver. So I set off once again along the Entangled Bank with no great expectations, but at least with the righteous feeling of someone doing his duty. Besides, it's important to grasp the idea that botanical events take place all through the year, whether you are out there botanising or back at home watching the football. The flowers may bloom in the spring but plants must have a botanical presence – and go through a botanical process – in every season or there wouldn't be any.

There were acorns crackling, crunching and rolling

underfoot as I set off, but I will allow you, as a bad botanist, to work out the identity of the big tree at the bottom of the lane. The bank was spotted red with hips and haws: the fruit of wild roses (rosehips) and hawthorns, the red colouring a come-and-get-me signal to passing birds ... so this was all very autumnal, that is to say, it was all about investment in the distant spring. There were also, when you looked a little more carefully, purple clumps of sloes, the fruit of the blackthorn bushes in the hedge, also waiting for birds ... but perhaps they would fall into the hands or bottles of humans wishing to add them to bottles of gin. (Gather sloes after the first frost, which breaks their skin, mix with half their weight in sugar, half-fill a bottle with the mixture, top it up with gin and leave it for two months, giving the bottle an occasional shake. After that, give the stuff away and buy a bottle of single malt.)

But there were still a few flowers visible along the lane, even if I found nothing new for these pages: white campions, one very small red dead-nettle, a cluster of bindweed flowers still hanging on. The ivy, holding tight to the trunks of the oaks, was luxuriantly in flower. Ivy flowers are not spectacular, small and greeny-creamy in colour, but they don't need to be: after the lushness of spring and early summer the competition had died away and ivy was the dominant flower. Late-flowering plants are in great demand from late-flying nectar-feeders, most obviously red admiral butterflies. There are many more insects on the wing later in the year these days, with killing frosts coming both later and fewer, and ivy helps them to survive.

That was about the lot for the Entangled Bank, but a couple of hundred yards further down the road there was a clump

of toadflax, and since it was a startlingly extravagant spec-
tacle for so late in the year, and since toadflaxes fascinated
both Linnaeus and Charles Darwin, I've made them honor-
ary members of the Entangled Bank, even though they were
pursuing their own struggle for existence on an Entangled
Triangle at the bottom of a quite different lane. After all,
what these two great scientists (and extraordinarily good
botanists) learned from these unexceptional flowers is of
major importance to all of us, botanists or not.

The toadflax colony looked like the corner of a cultivated
garden. That's partly because the blooms are relatively lavish
for a wild plant: one of those flowers of bilateral (rather than
radial) symmetry that we met in the previous chapter. They
are closely related to the garden plants called snapdragons
or antirrhinums. The flowers are pale yellow, picked out
with deep orange, and they bear a long spur. The nectar
and pollen are closed away by the curl of the petals, so that
it takes a strong insect – bee or bumblebee – to shove in and
take advantage of what the flower offers: a lavish supply of
nectar that encourages the visiting insect to seek out another
toadflax rather than dally elsewhere for lesser gain. The
closed flowers are (or were) used in a children's game: when
you squeeze the flowers they open, like a mouth, so you can
make the flowers talk.

Linnaeus, or Carl von Linné, was an eighteenth-
century Swedish scientist, one of the great thinkers of the
Enlightenment. He was a pioneer in the classification of life:
the study of who is related to whom. To make it all work in a
clear and logical way, he invented the binomial system: that
is to say, he gave everything two names. The rose that filled
the Entangled Bank with red hips is *Rosa canina*: the first bit

tells you it's a rose, the second name what species of rose. The generic name is *Rosa* and the specific name *canina*. Toadflax is *Linaria vulgaris*; generic names are always capitalised, specific names all lower case, and both should be in italics. (You use lower case even when the species in question is named for an individual human, thus the small Sri Lankan snake is *Boiga barnesii*, good name, though not, alas, chosen for me.) Linnaeus is the Latinised form of Linné, and it's not an affectation because he wrote in Latin. This was still the Western world's language of learning, and it was a convention that made knowledge available across nationalities. He published his findings under the title *Systema Naturae*. The first edition was a twelve-page thing published in 1735; by the time he had reached the twelfth edition he had listed 13,000 species of animals and plants, and though the business of naming and classifying is forever in flux, the Linnaean system is still essential to scientific understanding. The names and the issue of relatedness are important not just for the sake of order and tidiness, but for the understanding of how any ecosystem functions: ultimately, how the planet works.

And Linnaeus called toadflax 'monsters'. He did so because a neighbouring botanist in Uppsala found a colony of toadflax that wasn't quite right. The flowers had five spurs instead of one. A bad botanist wouldn't have noticed, but to a good one it was startling. Linnaeus wrote: 'This is certainly no less remarkable than if a cow were to give birth to a calf with a wolf's head.' He called the aberrant plants *peloria*: monster.

These monstrous toadflaxes weren't just interesting: they were deeply disturbing. How could a species produce wrong versions of itself? These five-spurred horrors hinted at a frightening and heretical view: that species weren't, after all, fixed, that a species could change – perhaps change so much that it could even form another species. The orthodox view, maintained by both religion and science, was that a species was immutable: that change was both impossible and inconceivable. It says in Genesis: 'And the earth brought forth grass, and herb yielding seeds after his kind.' It was as if the last three words were written in fire.

The Enlightenment was about the divorce between science and religion, between proof and faith, but it was a long, slow process, one that is by no means complete today. The toadflax asked a huge question: what if life was not static after all? What if life was, in fact, dynamic, ever-changing, forever renewing?

Darwin provided the answer a little more than a century later, as we have seen in the previous chapter. *Origin* was published in 1859 and a great deal of Darwin's subsequent work reinforced the conclusions he had reached in this volume: for example, his 1876 book *The Effects of Cross and Self Fertilisation in the Vegetable Kingdom*. It was a book largely inspired by toadflax.

Darwin never stopped trying things out. He was a great thinker, but he also loved a practical experiment. And he wrote: 'For the sake of determining certain points with respect to inheritance, and without any thought of close interbreeding, I raised close together two large beds of self-fertilised and crossed seedlings from the same plants of *Linaria vulgaris*. To my surprise, the crossed plants when fully grown were plainly taller and more vigorous than the self-fertilised ones.'

Plants go to considerable lengths to make sure they don't

fertilise themselves. Darwin was committed to the view that nothing evolves for no reason, and went to considerable lengths to find out why. He set up experiments on self- and cross-fertilised plants over eleven years. 'Cross fertilisation is sometimes ensured by the sexes being separated, and in a large number of cases, by the pollen [male] and stigma [female] of the same plant being matured at different times.'

He discovered that the problem of self-fertilisation is not just that a self-fertilised weak plant is likely to propagate itself as another weak plant: self-fertilisation is a bad thing even for a healthy plant. Darwin's conclusion makes it clear that sex is important, and that sex with non-related individuals is essential to producing vigorous and healthy offspring. Sex is important to toadflaxes, bumblebees, oak trees, deer and humans. Certainly, as we'll see a little later, it's possible for some species to propagate themselves without sex, but most can't hope to become an ancestor without an awful lot of it.

By grasping this essential fact of life, Darwin was moving towards an understanding of the recessive gene, and with it, the mechanism that makes evolution – evolution by natural selection – actually work. His failure to achieve a complete understanding of this mechanism troubled him: he was painfully aware that what he had come up with was just a nice idea – even if it was the only one that covered all the known facts. He had no idea that at the time that *Origin* was first astounding the world, a monk in Brno, in what is now the Czech Republic, was making the breakthrough that Darwin had longed for. The monk's name was Gregor Mendel and he was a great botanist. His most important work was done between 1856 and 1863, his study of the factors that govern inheritance was published in 1866 – and hardly a soul noticed. Darwin never even heard of him.

Mendel started off working with mice but his abbot thought it was unfitting for a monk to devote his life to mouse sex, so he switched to plants. He planted a couple of hectares with about 28,000 plants, almost all of them peas. He worked on seven different traits in different varieties of peas: height, pod shape and colour, seed shape and colour, flower position and colour. He made observations and from these he made a series of calculations of classic precision and beauty, so precise that subsequent scientists have suspected that he fiddled his results to make them fit so perfectly. Even if he did, the conclusions he drew were right.

He demonstrated that inheritance is not a simple matter of blending. If you cross a tall plant with a short plant, you won't get a load of medium-sized plants. You will get some tall ones and some short ones: three talls to one short, if tallness is what Mendel called the dominant 'factor'. Put one of the resulting shorts to another short plant and you will get some short plants – and some tall ones as well, if the factor for tallness is recessive. What he called factors we now call genes: Mendel created the science of genetics, a crucial area of modern research and, some say, crucial to the future of humanity. He proposed three laws of inheritance and they all stand to this day.

Coincidence, according to a character in Anthony Powell's *A Dance to the Music of Time*, is 'magic in action'. Mendel had, it seemed, been forgotten without trace, but in a two-month period of 1900, sixteen years after Mendel's death, three different researchers in three different countries rediscovered his work and replicated his experiments. More surprisingly still, all three acknowledged Mendel's priority. By the 1930s the work of Darwin and Mendel was accepted as the only coherent and fully valid explanation of the way that life operates. It has been called 'the modern synthesis', or sometimes, in a term demeaning to Mendel, 'neo-Darwinism'.

Botany is not a self-enclosed subject, a nice thing for people who happen to like flowers or have an eye for a tree. It gets to the heart of the big questions about who we are. Once you have learned to recognise a toadflax you will forever after be able, as you pass a pleasing yellow colony, to give a nod in passing to Linnaeus and Darwin; and every time you find a pea on your plate you can give another nod to Mendel. A bad botanist has an understanding of life unavailable to those who walk along an entangled bank without pausing.

Cedar of Lebanon

20

NAKED AND UNASHAMED
.

Pining for the pine tree
That ached for the sail

Robin Williamson of The Incredible String Band

There are only three native species of conifers in the UK, so you might think that identifying UK conifers is pretty straightforward. Not so: for reasons of usefulness, beauty or exoticism, we have imported many other species and that confuses things no end, at least for the bad botanist. Conifers – trees that bear cones – are gymnosperms, the bearers of naked seeds, as we have seen, while most plant species are angiosperms or flowering plants. Gymnosperms have just as much need for reproduction as angiosperms and have their own structures for producing and receiving pollen. These are sometimes, highly confusingly, called flowers, though they lack the defining attributes of real flowers. All conifers are pollinated by the wind: the more precise method of employing and paying insects and other animals to do the job is limited to the angiosperms (and by no means all of them, as we have seen). It follows that gymnosperms must produce a great deal of pollen if they are to have a decent chance of finding the receptive female parts of other trees.

Let's take a look at our three native conifers.

1. Scots pine

Scotland is a land of bare hills covered in sheep and deer: it comes as something of a shock to realise that this is a very recent phenomenon. These hills were once clad in Scots pines: tough trees that can take a great deal of cold without dying. But they were clear-felled to make charcoal for iron foundries and for their timber, which was used to build houses, and for the masts of ships, especially during the Napoleonic wars.

The felling came with the Highland Clearances of the eighteenth and nineteenth centuries, in which poor people were driven off the land so that sheep and later deer could be grazed there for the profit and pleasure of the rich. These two grazing species – with no wolves to keep them on the move – continued to make sure that any stray pine seedling that may sprout was at once nibbled out. The natural succession of vegetation has no chance in these unnatural circumstances.

But there are a few places where chunks of the ancient Caledonian Forest still stand, and are even being extended. Abernethy, run by the RSPB, is a forest full of Scots pines as they were meant to be, with red squirrels, capercaillies the size of turkeys and Scottish crossbills, birds with beaks perfectly engineered for the opening of pine cones, which they use to reach those naked seeds.

Scots pines grow naturally in lowland Britain as well as further north. They have also been widely planted, often for the timber and sometimes for their decorative nature. They do well on sandy soils and have been much planted along field margins in the Brecks, in Norfolk, and in Suffolk's sandling heaths, where they act as windbreaks and help to bind the soil, preventing wind erosion, the loss of topsoil from wind.

Scots pines often make a distinctive shape of a long, straight trunk with a flattish or roundish top; they can reach 35 metres and exceptional trees are even taller. But that's not something you can rely on, partly because trees are often pruned and shaped to human convenience and whim. The bark is reddish, at least in young trees; as they mature you're more likely to find grey-brown bark towards the bottom and redder stuff nearer the top.

Like most conifers, a Scots pine keeps its leaves – needles – all through the year. In this species the needles are ever-so-slightly twisted. Needles aren't as effective as, say, the massed leaves of an oak tree in midsummer when it comes to harvesting light, but they have advantages that oaks and other deciduous trees don't possess. They don't dry out in stressful conditions because each needle has a tough, waxy coat that retains moisture. They operate all year: a pine tree can take advantage of a bright winter day to make food, while the oak tree nearby is dormant. A pine tree has much less wind resistance than an oak in full leaf, so it's harder to blow down; a pine tree doesn't need to shed its leaves to withstand winter gales. And also, pine needles are very tough to eat, and few species do so. All this means that conifers are good at making a living in environments that would challenge broadleaf trees: they can take cold and snowy just as well as they can take hot and dry. The cones of Scots pines have a little stud in the middle of each scale. They are slow to develop and a tree will bear cones from this year as well as those mature cones from the previous year.

2. Juniper

We'll get on to gin shortly, but let's first celebrate the fact that the juniper has the most extensive range of any tree in the world, growing on both sides of the Atlantic and from Western Europe across to eastern Siberia. They're not generalists, and yet they grow well in wildly contrasting places in the UK. In the north of Britain they do best on cold, rainy sites with acid soil, and on heather-clad moorland. They often form the understorey of forests dominated by Scots pines. But down south they like hot, dry places, particularly water-starved chalk downlands. You mostly find them as shrubs or modest trees.

They seldom get higher than 10 metres, often much shorter. All the same, they can live for 200 years. They're slow growers: in the first seven years of their lives they won't get higher than 20 centimetres. They have grey-brown bark and reddish-brown ridged twigs. The needles have a single pale band on the top. The trees come in male and female form – most plants do both jobs, as we have seen – and the purple-black berries on the female trees are the stuff used for flavouring gin.

These are not technically berries but modified cones, these being gymnosperms. The berries used for flavouring gin distilled in this country are usually imported; it's a flavour that has never appealed to me, though I accept that I'm in the minority. The cones/berries are sometimes called bastard killers, for they were once consumed to bring about abortion; the combination of gin and a boiling-hot bath was used to bring about miscarriage before abortion was legalised. The wood burns with very little visible smoke. When laws were passed in the nineteenth century to make unregistered distilleries illegal, people burned juniper to fire the stills.

3. Yew

It's easy to recognise a yew: they're the conifers that grow in churchyards. Hundreds of churchyards in Britain and northern France come with their own ancient yew, a tree often older than the church itself. They are mostly smallish, usually around 10 metres, though twice that is possible. Yews have a red-brown bark with hints of purple in it, and small, straight needles, darker green above. Female trees bear bright red berries, which are actually modified cones called arils, open at one end.

It's often claimed that these churchyard yews mark sites that were sacred long before Christianity got there. How old do these trees get? Hard to say, because they don't grow with easily countable growth rings, as many trees do: they operate on a principle of constant replacement. The boughs become hollow, making accurate ageing still harder. It's probably fair to say that most churchyard yews are about 500 years old, and a good few of them twice that. There are some with extreme claims for great age, most famously the Fortingall Yew of Scotland, mentioned earlier, which is, some say, 9,000 years old, though 2,000 is a safer estimate.

Every part of the tree is poisonous apart from those arils, and they contain a poisonous seed. A more prosaic theory for their association with churchyards is that the fallen needles make the ground unsuitable for grazing, so they were planted as a keep-out. The wood from yews is good to work with, being the hardest of all the so-called softwoods. It also has an extraordinary elasticity: it's bendy and returns rapidly to its original shape. That makes it the perfect wood for archery: the yew long-bow was England's greatest-ever non-explosive weapon.

Those are all the native conifers we've got. There are many non-natives in Britain, grown for all kinds of purposes, but we'll take just three of them to represent the rest.

1. Sitka spruce

An island nation at war has an immediate and obvious problem of supply. Two world wars changed the look of Britain, for there was no option but to fall back on our own resources. Britain needed timber and had to use what was there already, since none could be shipped in. As a result, a lot of ancient forest, literally irreplaceable, was clear-felled. Some of this was then replanted with conifers selected for purely commercial reasons: trees that would provide timber for building and furniture. In the post-war years forestry became a national industry. There was a demand for plywood, thin sheets glued together with the grain at right-angles in alternate layers; and for board made from cellulose fibre, woodchip and adhesive. The trees are also used to make paper.

A dozen or so non-native species were planted to supply these needs, sometimes on the sites of ancient forest, sometimes on land that was poor for farming. The programme included areas of the New Forest, Thetford Forest and Kielder Forest. In the 1970s and 1980s, the government gave juicy incentives to people willing to finance the planting of non-native trees in the extraordinary blanket bog habitat of the Flow Country, in the north of Scotland. It was an ecologically damaging way of producing poor timber.

The favourite plantation species is Sitka spruce, which was brought in from North America and is named for the former Russian capital of Alaska, which was previously known as New Archangel. You can easily recognise Sitka spruce because it generally stands to attention in straight lines, each tree close to the next, making a dense canopy that doesn't allow anything to grow underneath. They can reach close to 100 metres in Alaska; in Britain they may make half that when given a free run. They carry distinctive cones, with serrated edges to each scale, and rather flattened needles.

Traditional commercial plantations aren't great for wildlife, any more than a field of oilseed rape, but they're used by red squirrels and Britain's smallest bird, the goldcrest. Some of these British forests in public ownership are now managed less intensively than they were in the past. A few years ago

I had the pleasure of going to Dunwich Forest in Suffolk to make the official release of twenty-nine Dartmoor ponies. They were introduced to roam and graze the forest, where native trees were recolonising after the felling of non-native conifers. The ponies are still there and doing a great job, opening up clearings and maintaining woodland rides. The wood is once again a nice place for wildlife and for humans.

2. Leyland cypress

Here is a rare non-dinosaur example of a biological entity more widely known by its scientific name than by any common name: these are the notorious leylandii, or to be formally correct, *Cupressus* x *leylandii*, though other versions of the name exist. The language of flowers is a complex and occasionally contradictory means of communication, but no one has any doubt that a red rose says love, rosemary says remembrance and leylandii says fuck off.

Leylandii are grown to shut people off from their neighbours, sometimes as an act of active aggression. The plant is a hybrid, a cross between Monterey and Nootka cypress, and it dates from 1888, when it was first grown at Leighton Hall in Wales. It continues to grow with classic hybrid vigour and with immense speed: a metre a year is the least you can expect and it can grow at that rate for a good fifteen years. It tolerates all kinds of soil, puts up with any amount of pollution and stands up well to exposure and wind.

It's more or less completely sterile, grown only from cuttings and it provides almost instant shelter, in the form of such varieties as Haggerston Grey and Leighton Green.

It is thoroughly unprepossessing, with a range of colours that lower the spirits and a texture like plastic: they look like monstrous versions of the toy trees enthusiasts add to model railways.

I was intrigued to discover another aspect of the story in correspondence with my old friend Lyn Sales. Her late husband, John, was head of gardens at the National Trust. He grew a leylandii hedge from cuttings propagated in a window box in West Kensington in 1959, perhaps the first such hedge in a small garden. It was much admired by a student of his who was setting up a nursery business. John passed on clippings from the hedge's twice-yearly trim; these were used as cuttings in the nursery and later sold on as plants. John wrote in his book *Shades of Green*: 'Mea culpa: am I really guilty of beginning the hideous rash of overgrown Leyland cypresses that have disfigured Britain for the past forty years? Like Dukas's Sorcerer's Apprentice, I was unaware of the force I had released!'

Leylandii hedges have been used so aggressively that they are covered under the 2003 Anti-Social Behaviour Act; in England and Wales you can ask local authorities to intervene in disputes about hedging – in practice almost always leylandii – and they have the power to reduce the height of the hedge. In 2001, Llandis Burdon, from near Powys in Wales (not far from Leighton Hall), was shot dead by his neighbour after an argument about the leylandii hedge between their two gardens.

There is a practice of growing random exotic conifers in gardens, largely because they don't take much looking after but at least look as if they have been put there on purpose. A friend of mine moved into a house that had just such a low-maintenance garden lavishly filled with conifers of all kinds of unlikely shapes and colours. He was planning to get them removed by contractors, but took the advice of a friend who told him: 'Buy a chainsaw instead. You'll save a fortune and have the time of your life.' The friend was right. The garden now looks great and Chris revelled in the weekends of destruction that made it possible.

3. Cedar of Lebanon

If the leylandii has its own unambiguous message, so does the cedar of Lebanon – and the message is grandeur. A tree with two or three centuries of growth is as imposing a thing as you will see anywhere, not just tall but with a huge circumference of low-to-the-ground horizontal, gravity-defying branches.

There were two or three on Streatham Common, not in the woodland but in The Rookery, the formal garden, on an open lawn that fell away sharply. There was one in particular that I loved: dominating at the top of the rise, with branches that grew an impossible distance from the trunk, which was divided into a series of lofty ascending columns. There was no chance of attempting to climb it in the busy, well-staffed place it was then, but I think I'd have regarded a climb as an act of blasphemy. It's gone now alas: a local organisation, The Friends of Streatham Common, told me it died in 2000, with a good couple of centuries on the clock. A couple more still survive.

Cedars of Lebanon were much planted by Capability Brown in the eighteenth century with his vision of what an

English landscape should look like: what he wanted was drama. Highclere Castle, now famous as Downton Abbey, borrows grandeur from its 300-year-old cedars. The species was introduced from the Eastern Mediterranean, as you would expect; there's one on the Lebanese flag, an indication of the tradition and meaning behind the tree. There are cedars of Lebanon in *The Epic of Gilgamesh*, one of the earliest of all written works, and naturally they turn up several times in the Bible: Psalm 92: 'The righteous shall flourish like the palm tree; he shall grow like a cedar in Lebanon.' You recognise these trees from their grandeur as much as any detail of needle and cone: their majestic forking into many trunks and their recklessly generous spread. After all, they inspired reverence in a ten-year-old.

Rosa spinosissima
'Falkland'

21

NAMING OF PARTS

... Japonica
Glistens like coral in all the neighbouring gardens,
And today we have naming of parts.

Henry Reed, 'Lessons of the War'

It's hard to be a polymath. They won't let you. Something catches your attention and you're inflamed with the desire to know more about it, so you look for a way in – and there isn't one. Even the most basic sources of information assume some kind of prior knowledge and experience: you, the absolute bedrock beginner, can't even get through the door. The insiders aren't actively hostile, but they live with a certain amount of knowledge, understanding and assumptions, and have no idea what life's like without them.

It's like joining a table when everyone's talking cricket. You happen to like the game yourself and would love to know more – but they're talking about Mankading and reverse

swing and the time Ben Stokes played the switch-hit off
Nathan Lyon and they might as well be speaking Mandarin.
It's the same with all kinds of potentially thrilling aspects of
life: you love music but you're not sure if Bach came before
or after Mozart and daren't ask. Or you've just started *Ulysses*
and it's thrilling but you've reached the third episode and
you're lost.

So this is the chapter that will, I hope, explain the botanical
equivalent of reverse swing, tell you that Bach came first,
that the Proteus episode is all about shape-shifting – and
that your own understanding is every bit as valid as mine
so relax and enjoy it.

Let's start with the notion that sex isn't everything.
Certainly, sex is of massive importance: almost all multicellular organisms go in for it, despite the huge costs involved.
We've already seen how plants go to great lengths to avoid
fertilising themselves – even though self-fertilisation
sounds like a hugely convenient idea. The reasons why
sex is so important are complex and controversial when
discussed at the genetic level, and lie beyond the scope
of this book and, for that matter, the understanding of its
author. But most of us are prepared to accept, on a purely
intuitive level, that sex matters and is the obvious way to
love and to make more of your own kind: so much so that
our greater wonder is reserved for organisms that can
reproduce without sex.

It happens in the animal kingdom – virgin birth, or
parthenogenesis, occurs in a good few species including
nematode worms, some bees, some scorpions and even a
few vertebrates, including occasionally birds, though never
us mammals. Birth without fertilisation by a male produces

a clone of the mother: her own genes are reproduced 100 per cent in her offspring.

Plants reproduce sexually by making seeds. This is made possible by the transfer of male pollen to the female stigma, and that gives the offspring 50 per cent of the genes of each parent. But many plants can also clone themselves by vegetative reproduction. I have already mentioned the bird table that became a willow tree. If left to their own devices, rather than tidied up, fallen willow branches often put down roots and become trees in their own right: genetically identical to the tree they fell from. Some tree species form a circle of descendants, as drooping branches reach the ground and become trees themselves. The ageing and central mother tree eventually dies, leaving a hollow ring of genetically identical offspring.

Many plants will put up a new and separate growth from their own roots. The English elm is particularly adept at this, and before the 1960s the farmed landscape of lowland Britain was dominated by hedgerows of elm, runs of genetically identical trees; you can regard these as one plant – one single organic entity. Would a greater diversity have helped the species to hold on in Britain when Dutch elm disease was accidentally introduced in the 1960s? Impossible to say. You still find elms in frequently cut hedges, but if they are allowed to grow proud of the hedge and reach a certain height, the lethal fungus invariably finds them out and they die. (The disease, incidentally, came to Europe from North America in imported bark; it was named for the Dutch pathologists who isolated the cause of the great dying.)

I can see an awful lot of reeds from my desk as I write these words: each underground stem – stolon – can put up

many above-ground stalks. Bulbs produce offsets of themselves. Some plants divide. A well-tended spider plant in
a living room produces long stalks with brand-new little
spiderlings at the tip: if the plant is growing naturally the
spiderlings find the earth, put down roots and become new
plants. A domestic plant-carer can snip off the plantlets and
allow them to flourish in a new pot.

Vegetative reproduction is part of the natural process,
and is much exploited by gardeners who want to make
more plants. At its most basic, this involves slicing a bit off
one plant – 'taking a cutting', as in the spread of leylandii –
and sticking it in the ground. If you want more certainty,
you put it in a pot and keep it safe, sheltered and warm, creating optimal conditions for the cutting to thrive – 'strike',
or put down roots – and become a plant in its own right.
You can dunk the cutting in hormone rooting powder to
encourage the process. As we have seen with some roses,
many domesticated plants are incapable of reproducing
sexually and must be propagated in nurseries by skilled
hands. Roses in gardens will often throw up new shoots
from below ground: observant gardeners cut these off as
soon as they are sighted. They are suckers, and will not
produce flowers like the main plant. That's because they
sprout from the rootstock; the plant you wish to encourage
to bloom has been grafted on top of this.

Grafting is a way of joining two plants together. The stuff
at the bottom is the understock and is usually chosen for its
resilience and vigour; the top part is the scion, selected for
its ability to produce fruit or flowers or whatever else pleases
the human grafters. As a general rule, this is with different
cultivars of plants that belong to the same species: the apple

tree in your garden will reject any attempt to graft, say, pears or cherries onto the original.

So what is a species? It's a key question for understanding almost anything in biology but it confuses people no end. Many intelligent and educated people aren't sure whether a Labrador is a species of dog (it's not, as we have seen – domestic dogs are all one species, the same species as wolf), whether cabbages and cauliflowers are different species of plants (they're not – more on this in a few paragraphs) and whether an egret is a breed of heron (it's not – it's a different species within the same family). A breed is a term used only for domestic animals. A rare breed of sheep is not the same thing as a rare species of wild animal. Humans could always breed more Jacob sheep if they chose; that's not the case with blue whales and giant pandas.

A species is a reproductive community, distinct from all others. Sex with a member of a different community – a different species – can't produce viable young. A horse and a donkey belong to different species. They can mate, with human intervention, and the result will be a mule – but all mules are sterile. You can't mate one mule with another, so they are non-viable. Reproductive communities can live side-by-side but be isolated by lifestyle: great tits and blue tits live in the same tree but they forage differently and show no sexual interest in each other. Neither will mate with the closely related African black tit or American chickadee, because they never see one: these species are additionally isolated by geography.

But these hard-and-fast boundaries can get fuzzy at the edges: humans may make the rules but we can't impose them. Many species consist of a number of subspecies, often isolated geographically. They may look slightly different and behave slightly differently; they may even be on their way towards becoming a new species. To add to the complexity, scientific opinion changes all the time. There isn't a holy book of species, in which every living thing is inscribed for all time: it's a living, happening and shifting business, contested and counter-contested. I was once part of an expedition with the Livingstone Museum in Zambia; we were trying to demonstrate that a small brown bird in an African forest was not a subspecies of neddicky but a good species in its own right. Alas, we failed to find the required evidence but later expeditions showed that Pearson's cisticola is indeed a true species.

In botany there is a level below that of subspecies. That is a variety, and it concerns small, subtle and often local differences within a wild breeding community. Zoologists don't use the term in the same way. It's also used informally and confusingly with plants in other contexts, and we'll get to that in a moment.

Sex can take place beyond the boundary of species, as with mules. Ligers, tigons and zonkeys (crosses between lions and tigers, donkeys and zebras) have been produced in zoos, though the practice is now regarded as frivolous. It can also happen in the wild: captive individuals of the New World species ruddy duck, kept in collections in the UK, got out and made their way to Spain. Once there, they started hybridising with the endangered white-faced ducks. These are considered a different species, but the young turned out to be perfectly viable. This process of hybridisation was considered a bad thing, and was stopped by a programme of eradication costing £5 million.

It succeeded in wiping out European ruddy ducks: sacrificed to the human belief in the sanctity of species. It was an extremely odd business.

We are more relaxed about cross-breeding plants – and plants hybridise in the wild with disconcerting eagerness. This has all kinds of intriguing possibilities for evolutionary biology. There are 909 recognised hybrids regularly found growing wild in Britain and Ireland, some of them producing viable offspring. There's even a book describing every one of them: *Hybrid Flora of the British Isles* by Christopher David Preston, Clive A. Stace and D. Pearman, and it's been put together by and for very good botanists indeed.

Humans can create cross-species hybrids by grafting one species to another or by cross-pollination – putting the pollen of one species to the stigma of another. These have to be fairly closely related if they are to take. You can't mate a liger with a tigon and get a viable hybrid, but you don't have to worry about that sort of thing with plants. If you can get a hybrid that works and grows well and does a job that humans want, you can often propagate it vegetatively. You don't buy leylandii seeds – you buy clones.

Many of the food plants that we grow from seed have a complex and often disputed history of hybridisation, and no one is sure what the parent species were. They got lost in the propagation: what matters is the food, not the ancestry; the agriculture, not the botany.

The process of plant-breeding works two ways. Sometimes a single species can be bred into many different forms: a wild *Brassica oleracea* is a leggy plant with flabby leaves and yellow flowers; from this one species we have bred red cabbage, green cabbage, white cabbage, Brussels sprouts, broccoli, cauliflower, kale, savoy cabbage, collard greens, kohlrabi and gai lan or Chinese broccoli.

Modern wheat comes from different hybridised species. And the process is constantly on the move: new kinds of plants – technically cultivars, but often confusingly called varieties – are always coming out, to please large-scale farmers or gardeners and allotment-keepers. A potato can be a Maris Piper, Rooster, Arran Pilot, Cara, Pink Fir Apple, Charlotte – and on and on. There are perhaps 5,000 potato cultivars. There are also about 150 different wild species, many of which have been cultivated and hybridised with others. They are bred for flavour, for their crop size, for their resistance to disease, for their tolerance of different conditions.

The way scientists allot names, on the binomial principle of Linnaeus, is straightforward enough once you've got the hang of it. The genus *Rosa* contains 300-odd species, all by definition closely related. One example, sometimes called Scotch rose, has the scientific name *Rosa spinosissima*. There is a Russian subspecies, so that gets an extra name: *Rosa spinosissima myriacantha*. There are many cultivars of this species: for example, the Falkland rose, which you write down formally as *Rosa spinosissima* 'Falkland'. There are also many rose hybrids, like *Rosa* × *canadensis*. So when you wish to set this down without any ambiguity whatsoever, you must use the right capitalisation, the right choice of roman or italic script (note that the '×' for the hybrid is written in roman in the middle of an otherwise italic name), and single quotes for the name of the cultivar – and now everyone knows *precisely* what sort of plant we are dealing with.

Creating good, effective cultivars is long, hard and

expensive work. It can take thirty years to create and test a good one. It follows that good varieties are treasured in the places where they are grown – and equally treasured in places where they were developed. Once developed they don't necessarily become part of the common store of human wealth: they can be patented. They are considered intellectual property, like this book. It's a process that puts agriculture under the control of the seed giants: if you are producing seeds that will lead to greater yield, greater tolerance of pesticides and a longer shelf life, you have something everyone wants. In the course of development, plants are sometimes bombarded with radiation to produce mutant versions, some of which turn out to be just what we want. And then of course we move into the vexed and complex field of genetic modification: the principal objection to this is the law of unintended consequences – we can't control what happens once the modified plants are exposed to the million variables of a living world.

Agriculture is increasingly a centralised and industrialised international business. We have an ever-growing human population and food supply is crucial, particularly when so much land is given up for the production of beef and dairy, which produce much less protein per acre.

The clash between traditional and modern industrial agriculture has given rise to what's called biopiracy. A classic example tells the tale best. In 1999 an American plant-breeder called Larry Proctor patented a bean cultivar and called it Enola, after his wife. Enola beans are damn good yellow beans and much cultivated, and that's because Enola beans were (and are) a traditional Mexican crop. But once the patent was granted, whenever Enola beans were imported into the United States, Proctor got royalties. The patent was revoked in 2009 and it's a lesson for all developing nations: look after your own.

I hope this chapter clarifies the business of the naming of plants. I am confident at least that one thing is made clear: when it comes to plants, humans have worked their will on them in many extraordinary ways across many centuries. Again and again and again we have made plants as we want them to be. We have done this to a far greater extent than we have with animals because plants are so much more biddable. We are in the process of creating our own botany: future generations will find out where this has taken our planet and its dominant species. All this may seem a long way off from identifying a lesser celandine on an entangled bank, but it's all connected by the chlorophyll that makes it happen and by the sun that drives the whole process.

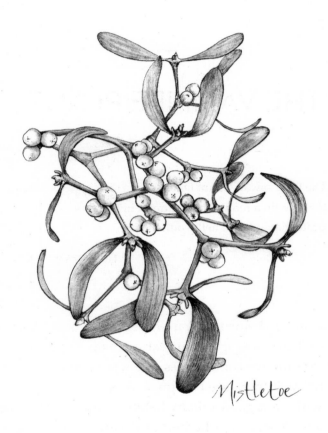

Mistletoe

22

THE VAMPIRE PLANTS

The last I saw of Count Dracula was his kissing his hand
to me, with a red light of triumph in his eyes, and a
smile that Judas in hell would be proud of.

Bram Stoker, *Dracula*

We are human beings, so you can't really blame us for behav-
ing like them – and it's in our nature to make morality plays
of everything we come across. We want good guys, so it is
essential that there are bad guys as well. No story is complete without a good villain: Satan, Widmerpool, Charlus,
Claudius, Dracula, Lex Luther, a roll-call of stepmothers and
Lord Voldemort. It follows that when it comes to botany we
have our good guys – roses, oak trees, wheat – and so we
must also have our bad guys. And often enough they take
the form of parasites.

The habit of using non-human life to make a series of
moral tales is as old as human speech, perhaps even older,

and they appear in every culture. We are a species of story-tellers, *Homo fabulator*, and parasitic plants – the whole idea of parasitism in any form – induces fear and loathing. It seems obvious that parasitic plants are wicked, and when I started to research this chapter, again and again I found them referred to as 'vampire plants'. It wasn't a reference to vampire bats, who feed on the blood of mammals and birds and do so without killing them. Rather it's about the cult of Count Dracula and other fictional undead humans who maintain their post-death existence by drinking the blood of living humans and quite literally sucking the life out of them. Dracula is a classic fictional villain – subject of Bram Stoker's 1897 novel – and he is called in to spice up our study of plants. So let us look at vegetative evil, as we humans perceive it.

1. Ivy

We'll start with the most obvious parasite of them all: a plant that strangles trees, sucks the life out of them Dracula-style and always ends up killing them. Or so it's widely assumed. The fact is that ivy is not actually a parasite. A parasite is defined by its ability to take water and nutrients from other plants, and ivy doesn't do that.

Ivy is a genus of a dozen or so species, native to Europe, North Africa and a good deal of Asia, introduced in many other places. (The American and Asian plant known as poison ivy, which causes contact dermatitis, is not related.) It is often found as a creeping plant, covering the ground, but when it gets a chance, it climbs. It does so using two methods: by producing its own glue and by clinging with fine root hairs. It will climb readily on anything it meets: rocks, houses, pylons, many other human constructions – and trees. This process gives it more room to develop and in many locations greater access to the light. Ivy can climb 30 metres above the ground, given time and a strong enough support, but remains rooted in the earth, from which it takes all its water and nutrients.

And it takes nothing from the supporting structure but support. Ivy can be regarded as a structural parasite, exploiting the strength and height of a tree, rock or building – but that's all it exploits. The plant clings but it doesn't penetrate the host plant's vascular system: it doesn't tap into the plumbing that transports water and nutrients about the plant. It is sometimes in competition with a tree-host for light, and also for the water and nutrients that both plants take from the soil through their separate root systems; it can be regarded as a burdensome weight for an old and dying tree. A tree with a great array of ivy in winter is more vulnerable to gales. Many tree surgeons will tell you that ivy damages a tree, while others strongly disagree. Certainly in normal circumstances, a healthy tree can host a sizeable ivy plant with very little inconvenience to itself.

Far from being a sinister anti-life strangler of good trees, ivy plays an important part in the ecosystems where it flourishes, as we have already seen, particularly as a late-season nectar source, most noticeably for red admirals. It also provides important shelter, as a densely growing evergreen, for overwintering invertebrates.

You will see, then, that I am keen to defend the ivy as an innocent victim: a good guy after all, falsely accused but in truth deeply noble, so once again I remind myself that nature is not there to teach us moral lessons. Its job is to be; parasitic species, no matter how sinister we think they are, have as much evolutionary validity as you and me.

There are many beliefs and traditions surrounding ivy but let's settle for just one: that ivy stops you getting drunk. A cup made from ivy wood, or even a drinking vessel with ivy pictured on it, is supposed to reduce the effects of alcohol. Pliny the Elder recommended ivy berries to bring about sobriety. Ivy was grown outside taverns: cause and cure all in one. You can drink any amount without ill effects if you have plenty of ivy, which is why Bacchus, the god of wine, is traditionally portrayed with an ivy wreath round his forehead.

2. Mistletoe

There's no ducking the fact that mistletoe is a genuine parasite: defined as a plant that gets some or all of its nutritional requirements from another plant. Mistletoe is a hemiparasite: it can photosynthesise and make its own food, but it also takes stuff from the plant it's growing on. All parasitic plants do this by means of a device that penetrates the host and links up to its vascular system, by way of the roots or the stem: the haustorium.

There are around 4,500 species of parasitic plants, or about 1 per cent of all, so it's not a weird aberration. Plant parasitism has evolved a dozen times over: it's a classic example of convergent evolution. It can be regarded as a natural and inevitable way of earning a living: as some plants take nutrients from the soil, others take them from a neighbour. It's a response to the availability of nutrients, not a moral choice.

Most of us will be familiar with mistletoe in two forms: as a green football at some inaccessible point in a mature tree, and as an aspect of Christmas decoration. It has oval leaves in pairs, small white flowers, and those waxy white berries that we take into our houses for mildly facetious kissing purposes. It has its favourite hosts – apple, lime, poplar, blackthorn, hawthorn and willow – but it's not much of a surprise to see a clump of mistletoe in any broad-leaved tree. They get planted there by birds, who pass the seeds out in their droppings, or wipe them – they're very sticky – off their beaks, where they adhere to the tree. Mistletoe stays green all through the year, and that makes the plants very visible in winter, when the host tree is standing leafless.

This apparent defiance of nature – a green plant growing without roots in a tree bereft of all other signs of life – was no doubt part of mistletoe's mystery and magical meaning. It has an ancient association with fertility – with the continuity of life in the darkest time of the year – and some claim that the white berries are reminiscent of semen. These ancient meanings have been transmuted into twenty-first-century jocularity and the kiss beneath the mistletoe. Traditionally, a request for a kiss in such circumstances could not be refused.

3. Dodder

As your eye gets accustomed to straying towards plants, you will occasionally notice an anomaly: a plant, usually gorse, wrapped up in an irregular net of reddish threads. These threads are dodder, and it's highly disconcerting to realise that it's a plant. Not part of a plant but the whole thing. This goes against everything that we understand about plants: it doesn't have roots or leaves and it isn't even green. It doesn't need to be. You only need chlorophyll – the stuff that makes a plant green – if you're going to photosynthesise and dodder doesn't bother. It doesn't make its own food: it takes all it needs from other plants.

It is, then, a complete parasite: a holoparasite, a plant that can live in no other way and has no back-up plan. It's a parasite or it's nothing. There are about 200 species, and they're found all over the temperate and tropical parts of the planet. The most common British species, referred to simply as dodder, mostly parasitises gorse, but will turn to heather and wild thyme. The related greater dodder prefers nettles.

Dodder germinates in the soil as most plants do, but as soon as it has done so it's in a race: it has to find a host within a week or die. It picks up chemical clues in the air and grows towards their source: in other words, to a highly limited extent, the plant has both sense and movement; you might almost say volition. When it has found a host it sets about producing haustoria: the invasive organs that eat into the host plant and allow the parasite to operate. Once it's done that, it abandons its roots and grows on its unwilling host. The plant has a slew of informal names: strangleweed, scaldweed, wizard's net, devil's guts, hellbine, love vine, angel hair and witch's hair.

Dodder produces flowers and fruit, visible to the observant botanist. The leaves have been reduced to tiny scales. The roots have been done away with. There is no extravagant structure to catch the light: this is a pared-down, slimline living machine that has simplified itself to a point of perfect minimalism. With plants like dodder, we must set aside the notion that evolution is a constant drive towards improvement, increased sophistication and ever-greater complexity. Most parasites, animals and plants both, take the exact opposite route, rising from complex ancestors to become thrillingly simple and utterly modern life forms. Evolution is no snob: if the answer to the question of how to become an ancestor lies in simplicity, then living and evolving organisms will tend towards simplicity. Dodder is as much an evolutionary masterpiece as a cheetah, an eagle, an oak tree, every plant that grows on an entangled bank – and of course, you and me.

4. Yellow rattle

I have tried to show you an out-and-out parasite as a plant that's not really a villain, so it's high time I offered you the parasite as hero. So here is the Robin Hood of parasites, the parasite that stands up for the underdog, the parasite that steals from the rich to give to the poor. Here is yellow rattle.

You could walk past a spreading colony of yellow rattle and never suspect anything even remotely sinister, let alone parasitic. Yellow rattle looks like a particularly bright and cheerful wildflower, usually in a flowering meadow, one of the most fragile, treasured and damaged habitats in Britain. The flower is, unsurprisingly, yellow, rather tube-like, at the end of a chunky green calyx, the bit that comes between the flower and the stalk. When the flowers are gone there are longish brown seedheads, and when you tap them, they rattle – so the plant is yellow and it rattles, but not at the same time. It stands on a longish, rather bare stem, and is in flower mostly between May and July, though it can hang on into September.

And it's a hemiparasite: it gets some of its nutrients by parasitising the roots of grass. This weakens the growth of the grass, and that's good news for other plants. With gaps in the once-suffocating blanket of grass there are opportunities for other plants – and so a community of meadow flowers is made possible by the depredations of the parasite.

The presence of yellow rattle was once a bad sign, spelling out the fact that your grazing meadow was losing its richness. These days a great deal of grassland is managed with selective herbicides and pesticides, to make it a monoculture of ryegrass. But when a meadow is managed for wildlife conservation, the hero-parasite of yellow rattle is introduced on purpose: it weakens the grasses and opens the door for many other different species, so you end up with that rare and glorious thing, a flower-rich meadow. Many people now deliberately introduce yellow rattle into their back-garden lawn, turning it into a small but lovely meadow.

5. Sundew

Dracula is a name given to plants that feed on other plants, but we have no name bad enough for plants that eat animals. Carnivorous plants are not parasites, but like parasites they are not by any means self-sufficient. And they hold a strange fascination for us – as if they were not just unnatural but in some kind of cosmic way wrong. Linnaeus was disturbed by them because they didn't fit in with his view of world order; as a result he believed that the Venus flytrap was not eating the insects but sheltering them from the rain. Darwin was thrilled by them for the same reason – or rather, because they did fit in with his own revised view of the way life works. He published *Insectivorous Plants* eleven years after *Origin*.

Carnivorous plants are not restricted to remote tropical locations: there are several species in this country, including two or three in the sundew family. A sundew seems to carry big drops of dew on its leaves even in the heat of a sunny day – but they're not dewdrops, rather a lethally sticky liquid that traps insects, the better to devour them. The plant responds to the touch of an alighting insect with movement: moving hairs trap the insect beyond any possibility of escape. After that the entire leaf curls around it so that it can be digested: it's another plant with both sensitivity and the power of movement. Once caught, the insect dies of exhaustion or asphyxiation, normally within fifteen minutes. There are a couple of hundred species of sundews – *Drosera* – across the world; the one most often found here is the round-leaved sundew. It has reddy-green leaves covered in hairs, and they grow in a rosette around the base. The plant produces white or pink flowers in season: not the most memorable thing about it.

They grow in wet, acidic places, among sphagnum moss at the edge of boggy pools and on wet heathland and moorland. These aren't attractive places to most plants because making a living here is tough: not enough nitrogen and other nutrients. But – and it was Darwin who nailed this – if you can catch and devour insects you can use the nutrients they contain for your own purposes.

The consumption of animals is not necessarily sinister in itself: humans have been doing it for most of the existence of the species. Robins and blue tits, beloved birds, mostly survive by eating insects. But the idea of a plant doing so makes us queasy. It destroys the ancient ideas of the *scala naturae*: the idea that everything works in a hierarchy, a kind of pyramid, with us a level below the angels and a modest two levels below God – but certainly above everything else that lives on Earth, just as all animals are above all plants. Plants that eat animals contradict that atavistic world view, which is why they bothered Linnaeus and delighted Darwin.

The idea of actively hostile plants fills us with horror. The most famous fictional exploitation of this terror is John Wyndham's 1951 novel *The Day of the Triffids* – and to this day, people who have never read the novel or seen the 1963 film refer to any strange and apparently threatening plant as a triffid. The same terror was given a more jocular treatment in *Little Shop of Horrors*, in which people were eaten by a plant called Audrey II.

Deadly nightshade

23

THE GARDEN OF DEATH

No, no, they do but jest, poison in jest; no offence i'
th' world.

Shakespeare, Hamlet

We humans have altered plants, animals and a great deal of
the planet to make eating a more straightforward business ...
so much so that we have forgotten that most living things
regard being eaten as counter-productive and have evolved
all sorts of ways of avoiding it. Under normal circumstances
animals run away or hide or even fight back, prompting the
French rhyme:

> *Cet animal est très méchant;*
> *Quand on l'attaque il se défend.*

Vladimir Nabokov translated this:

This animal is very wicked,
Just see what happens when you kick it.

Most plants resent the idea of being eaten just as much as any *méchant* animal. So naturally – the *mot juste* if ever there was one – they have evolved ways of avoiding this calamity. Sometimes, as we have seen, being consumed is useful, most obviously when seeds are encased in tasty fruits and get dumped in places far from the mother tree after the fruit has been consumed, and also in the floral offerings of nectar and pollen. But in the main, being eaten is a thing to be avoided, and if total avoidance isn't possible, then minimising the attack is a very sound plan. We are accustomed to thinking of predators as creatures that predate other mammals, or birds, and at a stretch, insects and other invertebrates. But if you look at it from a plant's point of view, wandering vegetarians are a constant existential threat and anything you can do to stop them treating you as a square meal is a sound strategy. Plants have predators and we humans can be numbered among them.

Plants have one very great disadvantage when it comes to avoiding predation: they can't run away. This gives us the wrong impression that they are passive: that they take their consumption philosophically, as part of the day's work, as part of their lot of suffering. But plants not only do a great deal to avoid being eaten; like the *méchant* animal, many are very well equipped to fight back.

Some plants have developed an armoury of thorns and spines and thick fuzzes and furs to put predators off: like the hunted stag in C. S. Lewis's *Narnia* story *The Silver Chair*, they tell potential predators: 'I'm tough, you won't like me.' Acacia trees in the African savannahs have evolved alarmingly long thorns: giraffes in turn have astonishingly tough mouths to combat them, though acacias are safe from most other browsing species. It's a classic evolutionary arms race.

The best and most widespread defensive systems in plants rely on chemistry rather than physics. We tend to think that poisonous plants are unusual and sinister, a deeply disturbing variation from the norm. Our atavistic human fear of poisonous plants is exploited brilliantly in Ian Fleming's novel *You Only Live Twice*, in which James Bond must enter a garden that his arch-enemy Ernst Stavro Blofeld has planted entirely with poisonous plants. It's described in a chapter entitled 'Slay it with flowers'.

Fleming writes about poison in plants as something exotic, and Blofeld's garden of poisonous plants comes across as shockingly perverse. But you can establish a poison garden yourself with very little trouble. A trip to your local garden centre will give you all you need, and you won't raise an eyebrow when you take your trolley up to the checkout ... you may even have just such a garden already. All you need to do is plant hydrangea, oleander, daffodil, wisteria, foxglove, lily of the valley and rhododendron – and you have an English suburban version of Blofeld's Garden of Death.

But perhaps you prefer to grow vegetables. You'd think you'd be safe from poisonous plants in a kitchen garden. But vegetable gardeners deal with poisonous plants all the time: potatoes, tomatoes and aubergines are all poisonous, as you would expect from members of the deadly nightshade family. Every part of a potato plant is poisonous apart from the tubers, the modified stems used for storing nutrients, which are the bits that we consume with such delight. Even these tubers can contain poisons, so don't eat the green bits. Potato plants have gone to a great deal of evolutionary trouble to avoid being eaten, but in recent centuries they have conquered much of the earth by virtue of the only non-poisonous part they possess. It turned out that edibility was their strength all along.

The creation of chemicals designed exclusively for defence is an expensive investment. If you don't come under attack, you've gone to a lot of trouble for nothing. To avoid this waste of resources, some plants wait until an assault is imminent before manufacturing their poisons. This is a smart way of operating, but it depends on an early-warning system, and some plants have developed one. When one tree in a forest is attacked, it informs the other trees and they all set about making poison. The messages are passed in chemical form along the network of underground fungi that links the trees. This network is not made from the fruiting bodies that we are familiar with and called mushrooms and toadstools: this is the mycelium, the threads from which they spring. The soil is full of mycorrhizal fungi: many fungi live in and around the roots of trees. The fungi exploit the trees and are in their turn exploited by the trees as a messenger service. The trees really can talk to each other.

This may be a little New Age for your taste, but the principle and practice have been demonstrated in laboratory conditions. Broad beans linked by fungus have been observed informing each other when one of their number is under attack by aphids. The plants that have not been attacked then produce the chemicals needed to repel the aphids, and are ready when they arrive. Those without the fungal link failed to do so.

Poisons affect different species and different individuals within a species in different ways. In humans a peanut is an excellent source of protein to many but is lethally dangerous to some. Intolerance of alcohol was largely bred out of Western humans because brewing was the preferred method of keeping water safe to drink; those that couldn't tolerate alcohol tended to not survive and become ancestors. But in China people preferred to make water safe by boiling it and drinking it as tea, so alcohol intolerance is far from rare in Chinese societies. We are accustomed these days to people who have varying degrees of intolerance to lactose and gluten. It follows that many berries that are distasteful, unpalatable or damagingly poisonous to many mammals are not the slightest problem to birds, who are likely to carry the seeds much farther from the mother tree than a mammal.

There are also advantages in being selectively poisonous. Apples, particularly the seeds, contain amygdalin, which is a mixture of sugar and cyanide. Chewing apple seeds releases this, though in small doses that don't actually kill a human. They pass right through a digestive tract if unchewed, and do so safely: their shape helps them to whizz through. A well-chewed meal of about 100 grams of apple pips might be enough to kill you. Other fruit stones and pips that contain cyanide include almonds, greengage, apricot, cherry, peach, plum, pear and nectarine: it's a defence mechanism that gives them the best possible chance of reaching the ground, germinating and eventually becoming an ancestor tree.

Rhubarb is another much-eaten poisonous plant. The stalks are safe, but the leaves contain a good deal of oxalic acid. You'd have to consume about 5 kilos of leaf to die from rhubarb, but a badly prepared dish can cause mouth-burning, nausea, diarrhoea, eye pain, foul-smelling urine and fever.

It comes as a mild surprise – at least to me – to learn that brassicas (cabbage and the rest) are not poisonous to humans, but they can be damaging to mammalian livestock. They contain toxic compounds which repel many species of invertebrate plant-eaters, though by no means all, as any gardener will tell you. Greenfly, caterpillars of the various species of white butterflies, nicknamed 'cabbage whites', and cabbage fly larvae all feed on brassicas and thrive. The caterpillars of large white butterflies do more than just put up with the poisons: they keep hold of them and use them for their own protection. The sequestration of plant toxins is far from unusual: species that take a positive advantage from the poisons they consume.

A classic British example of sequestration is the cinnabar moth. As we've seen, the caterpillars live on ragwort; they also absorb the toxins. These caterpillars are easy to find: you will sometimes find a ragwort plant swarming with bright black-and-yellow creatures visible from a fair old distance. Black and yellow is a warning: keep off, I'm dangerous. Cinnabar moth caterpillars profit from the poisons they consume by becoming dangerous beasts in their own right. The adults retain the toxins, handsome creatures of red and bottle-green. Other British species that work the same trick include European pine sawfly, turnip sawfly, cabbage aphid, death's-head hawkmoth, garden tiger moth, ragwort flea beetle and seven-spot ladybird.

The chemical defences of plants have often been put to human use. We have already seen how aspirin was developed from the defence mechanism of willows. Other examples: caffeine in the coffee plant, theobromine in the cacao plant that gives us chocolate, morphine from poppies, nicotine from the tobacco plant, cocaine from the coca plant, tetrahydrocannabinol in cannabis and, from the rosy periwinkle of Madagascar, vinblastine which is used in the treatment of Hodgkin's disease.

The chemical defence of plants is a wide-ranging, complex and nuanced business, resistant to any easy attempt to seek out heroes and villains. Let's take a look at some of the most toxic plants we are likely to come across on a pleasant walk in the countryside of Britain and Ireland.

1. Deadly nightshade

This is a member of the family of Solanaceae that comprises up to 2,700 species and includes, as we have seen, potato, tomato and aubergine. The plant that concerns us here is a bushy perennial that grows up from the ground fresh every year and produces multiple branches. Its leaves are pale pointed ovals, the flowers purple-brownish bells, which have an appropriately sinister look to them – at least, they do when you know the name of the plant. The berries are shiny black and rather attractive: it's been said that three of them are enough to kill a child. They dry out the mucous membrane of the mouth and throat, dilate the pupils, and speed up the heart, and they cause hallucination and death.

But extracts have been used as a stomach sedative, and the plant has also been used as a cosmetic, to dilate the pupils of the eye so that the wearer appears aroused and therefore more attractive. The scientific name for the plant is *Atropa belladonna*; Linnaeus, who came up with it, was referring to the practice of applying juice from nightshade berries to the eyes for this sexy effect. Cleopatra used juice from the related henbane, as well as those rose petals, when she was seducing Mark Antony. Henbane grows in Britain; Dr Crippen used scopolamine, a drug synthesised from henbane, to kill his wife in 1910.

2. Foxglove

We have already met the foxglove on the Entangled Bank: it's a poisonous plant and every part of it is toxic. It is also the source of one of the most important heart treatments available, used to control irregular heartbeat. How did they know? How did they find out? This is one of the eternal questions of medicine. In the eighteenth century, a physician called William Withering used foxgloves for the successful treatment of what was then called dropsy: swelling formed by congestive heart disease, these days referred to as oedema. He wrote this up for the Royal Society. Erasmus Darwin, grandfather of Charles, also used the plant successfully, and there was a bitter row about priority.

But where did they get the idea from in the first place? Either of them? Where did the notion come from that a plant full of dangerous poisons would be just the job when it came to curing heart patients? The answer lies in ancient and often clandestine traditions of herbal medicine. Herbal remedies were often kept secret because too great a wisdom led to accusations of witchcraft. The Dutch Jesuit theologian Martin Delrio said, in his six-volume work *Investigations into Magic* (1599–1600): 'It is evidence of witchcraft to defend witches.' It's been estimated that in Europe, in the three centuries to 1750, between 40,000 and 100,000 people were executed for witchcraft. There was considerable incentive to keep quiet about curative herbs.

Digitalis is the active substance in foxgloves and it contains several compounds. One of these, digoxin, is used today in a synthesised form as a successful treatment for heart disease. It's worth noting that a good half of our medicines came originally from nature. There are many more untested species out there; we've hardly scratched the surface. It's likely – perhaps statistically inevitable – that plants with potentially life-saving properties go extinct every day.

3. Hemlock

Hemlock is a common enough plant of roadsides and I was unlucky or unobservant not to find it in the course of my peregrinations along the Entangled Bank. It's a tall umbellifer, often waist-high and can reach 2 metres. It could easily be confused, at least by a bad botanist, with cow parsley. Look for purple blotches on the stem as well as an unpleasant smell.

It's a classic villain-plant, with nicknames that include devil's bread and devil's porridge. Its poison effectively deters grazing mammals, from rabbits to cows, and affects most other mammal species, including humans. The seeds and roots are especially poisonous: a period of apparent drunkenness is followed by respiratory collapse and death within seventy-two hours. There is no antidote.

Socrates is regarded as the first great moral philosopher of the Western tradition and was the teacher of Plato. He was found guilty of impiety and corrupting the minds of Athenian youth and had to choose between recantation and death. He chose the latter, selecting death by hemlock. Keats turned to the plant in *Ode to a Nightingale*, with one of the better pairs of opening lines:

> *My heart aches, and a drowsy numbness pains*
> *My sense, as though of hemlock I had drunk.*

Agatha Christie, as much fascinated by gardens as by murder (she ran a small nursery business), had many poisoning episodes in her extensive oeuvre of death and detection. In her short story *Five Little Pigs* the murderer uses hemlock as his murder weapon. He is found out, of course, by Hercule Poirot.

4. Monkshood

This is perhaps the British all-comers champion: the most virulently poisonous plant routinely growing in Britain and Ireland. It comes as a surprise to learn that it's much planted in gardens, along with its equally poisonous relatives like winter aconite. Monkshood grows wild in woods and along ditches and it throws out attractive bluish-purple flowers; the name is helpful as the flowers have a monk-like cowl over them. They grow on erect stems surrounded by jagged leaves. The plant has an impressive collection of folk names, including wolfsbane, leopard bane, mousebane, and even women's bane, along with devil's helmet and queen of poisons.

The wolfish name is also found in Ancient Greek: *lycoctonum*, which also means wolf's bane, a bane being a source of harm. Poison extracted from monkshood was used to tip the arrows used for hunting wolves. It is an acute neurotoxin; when taken in large doses, death for humans is said to be almost instantaneous. Professor Snape mentions monkshood in the first of the *Harry Potter* books.

The genus *Aconitum* contains 250 or so species, which are native to much of the northern hemisphere. They have been used in herbal medicine for centuries and are a part of traditional Chinese medicine. The plant is mentioned by Theophrastus and Pliny the Elder, and there is a theory that Socrates was killed by monkshood rather than hemlock: all one to him, I should imagine. Aconite is a standard remedy in homeopathic medicine, and is used to treat anxiety as well as fever, headache and some other conditions. It was used in Western medicine until the middle of the twentieth century. In 2021, Sadyr Japarov, president of Kyrgyzstan, promoted aconite as a cure for Covid. As a result at least four people were taken to hospital.

5. Cuckoo pint

Like the foxglove, this plant also grows along the Entangled Bank, and like the foxglove we must look at it again, this time as a poisonous plant. All parts of the plant, especially the red berries, contain sharp crystals that can be damaging when eaten. The berries are harmless to birds, who do much of the seed distribution. Cuckoo pints seldom claim human victims because consumption is so unpleasant: instant burning of the skin of the mouth, the tongue and the throat, difficulty breathing, considerable pain ... there isn't much incentive to keep on eating them. They can be dangerous to cats and dogs.

There's a persistent but false belief that cuckoo pints also poison and devour insects. The male flowers lie hidden from easy sight, insects that clamber down to seek them get trapped by stout hairs. They get covered with pollen, but they then escape – and if all goes well, they fly to another cuckoo pint and offload the pollen on the female flower.

6. Giant hogweed

This plant is not deadly poisonous and can't be considered a rival in any way to the others in this chapter, but it's both spectacular and notorious and so it shoves its way in, as is its wont. It's not native to Britain: it was brought in from the Caucasus Mountains in the nineteenth century as an ornamental plant, mostly because it's so wonderfully dramatic. It doesn't seem right that a flower – that is to say, a stalk with a flowerhead on top – should be so big.

It looks like a giant cow parsley and is a reasonably close relation, along with carrot and parsley. It can easily reach 3 metres, sometimes higher, with a 2-metre spread. The flowerheads alone can be 60 centimetres across; and the leaves can be 3 metres long and 1.5 metres wide. For a plant that must grow afresh each year, it's colossal.

It doesn't poison: it burns. Or rather, it makes the sun burn you. The sap makes the skin hyper-sensitive to sunlight: the sun then burns and causes blisters; these can recur for months, even years. I once had a neighbour who allowed giant hogweed to flourish in his garden, and it towered over our shared fence. He boasted that it was illegal; not strictly true, but local authorities can cause you to remove them if they are considered a nuisance. Perhaps I should have fought back with a leylandii hedge.

Pyramidal
orchid

24

SEX AND PASSION

Lord Illingworth told me this morning that there was an
orchid as beautiful as the seven deadly sins.

Oscar Wilde, *A Woman of No Importance*

Flowers are about sex; orchids are about passion. The sexual
lives of orchids are elaborate, complex, mysterious and
sometimes perverse. They are associated in our minds with
human passions of an exotic, expensive and not entirely
healthy kind. They are plants that excite frenzy in those
that seek them: the rare orchids of Britain are hunted – and
guarded – as if they were doubloons and pieces of eight. For
some people botany is a nice way of spicing up a nice country
walk; for others it's an addiction worth crossing the country
for, to go through any kinds of discomfort for, to feel jealousy,
rage and joy for.

The very idea of British orchids took me aback when I
was first aware of it. I thought orchids were strictly tropical,

found only by intrepid climbers in the rainforest canopy or grown by fanatics in hothouses, to be purchased by wealthy men as gifts for their ruinously expensive mistresses. They were flowers for the decadent, flowers for the thrillingly depraved. Inevitably they crop up in that great celebration of perversity, *À rebours* (translated as *Against Nature*) by J. K. Huysmans: 'Once he was alone again, he surveyed the great tide of vegetation that had flooded into his entrance-hall, the various species all intermingling, crossing swords, creeses, or spears with one another, forming a mass of green weapons, over which floated, like barbarian battle-flags, flowers of crude and dazzling colours ... Yes, his object had been achieved: not one of them looked real.'

When a young man, Marcel Proust was painted with a cattleya orchid in his buttonhole, as barbaric a battle flag as you could wish for. Later, in the first volume of his masterpiece *À la recherche du temps perdu*, Odette's corsage – also a cattleya – is disturbed when the horses pulling her carriage are spooked. Her companion Swann takes charge: 'Look, there is a little – I think it must be pollen, spilt over your dress – may I brush it off with my hand?' He would have been more correct to say 'pollinia' but never mind, the lady assents to his brushing, he brushes with all the attention one would expect – and before long they are referring to the act of love as 'doing a cattleya'.

There are many of these fabulous foreigners, but there are also, it is usually agreed, fifty-two species of orchids growing wild in Britain, some of them, to those with a good botanical eye, relatively common, others mind-blowingly rare, all of them really rather extraordinary – and capable of exciting the passions of good and bad botanists alike.

I first heard about the passion for hunting British orchids from *Daniel Martin* by John Fowles. It's a fascinatingly flawed novel, but very sound on orchids. Daniel and Anthony are both students at Oxford; Daniel enters Anthony's room and finds him painting an orchid in a jam-jar of water. A man orchid, in fact, but more of that species in a moment. They are very different people, but bond over the orchids because it's a shared passion, and the sort of thing, apparently, that you only discuss with fellow initiates. 'I had in my teens fallen prey a little to the orchid mystique.'

They pair off with two sisters and go on botanical forays: 'In our orchid-hunting I never really rose above the role of shikari – I found the game, he shot it. The thrill for me was finding the rare ones – my first (and last, alas) Monkeys near Goring, a solitary Fly under a sunshot whitebeam at the edge of a Chiltern beechwood. His heaven was a wet meadow full of dull old Dactylorchids: counting and measuring and noting down the degree of hybridisation. I wanted to find the flowers; he wanted to establish a new subspecies. I lived (and hid) poetic moments; he lived Druce and Godfery.'

One of the great pleasures of British orchids is their subtlety. Most of them are not obvious: neither to find nor to appreciate. It takes a little bit of practice, a little bit of insider knowledge to be aware of their loveliness. They're not like the tropical orchids – the cattleya for example – that trumpet their gorgeousness to the world. A non-botanist is perfectly capable of walking past an orchid, or even a colony of orchids, without really noticing them, and for that matter, so is a botanist as bad as me. But even I have improved, and once you've got your eye in, you will have earned the right to say, 'these are beautiful flowers, if you but knew it'.

James Bond was scathing about an orchid, autumn lady's
tresses, which M was painting. He enters M's home on
Christmas Day – this is Ian Fleming's novel *On Her Majesty's
Secret Service* – to find him hunched over 'an extremely
dim little flower in a tooth-glass'. But it's a thing of beauty
and wonder to those who know. M compares it to tropical
orchids: 'How in hell can a man like those disgusting flowers? Why, they're damned near animals, and their colours,
all those pinks and mauves and the blotchy yellow tongues,
positively hideous.'

Nature, of course, isn't striving to please human eyes, not
even M's, though many species have profited from their ability to do so: our gardens are full of them, while species that
give us less pleasure are dug out or poisoned and disparaged
as weeds. Sometimes evolution brings us species that look
beautiful to human eyes (leopard, golden eagle and, if you're
not James Bond, autumn lady's tresses) and just as often, species we find ugly (hyena, lappet-faced vulture, and the giant
tropical parasite of jungle vines called rafflesia).

One of the pleasures of becoming a bad botanist is the way
that your eye for detail gets sharpened: the more you look,
the more you see. Recognising a wild orchid brings delight
in your improved eye and an equal or greater delight in the
beauty of what you see. I remember the first orchid I found
for myself: a southern marsh orchid (an example of what
Daniel Martin called 'dull old Dactylorchids', though these
days he'd refer to them as a *Dactylorhiza*). I dropped to my
knees, not in prayer but to get a proper view of the damn
thing, and there I found joy in miniature: a stalk a few inches
long topped by a spike of quietly gorgeous pink flowers, each
one marked with subtle spots and speckles in a darker shade.

The plant was lovely enough as it was, but also, well, it was an orchid. That lifted it above the common run, as if it was a species of eagle or big cat. Here was the soul-deep thrill of being in the presence of something special.

There are 28,000 species of orchid worldwide, so when we look a little more closely at their eccentric way of making a living, we have to accept that no matter how odd it may seem, it works extremely well. Orchids have a unique strategy when it comes to making seeds: they produce them in astronomical numbers. They are able to do so because they don't supply the seed with anything remotely useful: they all lack the protein-filled starter-pack that most seeds possess. Normally a seed comes equipped with what it needs to germinate: a food supply that will tide it over until it's able to photosynthesise and make food for itself. That's why so many seeds make good food for animals – think of a broad bean or a Brazil nut: when we eat them we steal the food that has been allocated by the parent plant to its offspring. There's no point in eating an orchid seed, which is a plus point for the plant. They must therefore be spread by the wind, since they can't use animals as intermediaries. There are so many of them that the chances of a few of them landing in just the right spot are pretty high, even in today's reduced world. But once they land in such a place, they have no resources of their own.

This is a trait that added greatly to the orchid mystique: for many years no human could make them grow from seed. It's very, very hard to make more orchids unless you're an orchid yourself. No one could work out how to do it. The answer is fungi: the thin threads of mycelium that are the essential living and working parts of any fungus. The fallen orchid seed may have no food of its own, but it can establish a relationship with mycelium, take nutrients from it and use them to germinate. Many species continue to steal from fungi throughout their lives – and this explains why they are able to thrive in nutrient-poor and light-poor habitats. In other words, part of the orchid mystique comes from the fact that they often grow – not only grow but thrive in lush and glorious forms – in places where no flower should be. Many tropical orchids grow as epiphytes, plants that grow on other plants; I am familiar with the lavish leopard orchid that grows on branches in the wooded savannahs of Africa, and it's as gorgeous as the mammal it was named for.

All these traits helped to make them objects of desire. They were hunted and traded extensively. In the nineteenth century the most desired specimens were sold for extraordinary sums: there's a record of a single specimen going for £325, about £100,000 today. The passion for the beauty and the prestige of orchids has been called orchidelirium. The breakthrough with human cultivation of orchids didn't come until 1922, when it was discovered that the growing medium could be injected with nutrients that mimicked those obtainable naturally from mycelium. Now you can buy a pretty funky orchid at your local supermarket, and it won't cost you £100,000, or even £325.

The system of tiny seeds in superabundance means that a plant needs a very great deal of pollen to make them. The flowers attract pollinators in the time-honoured way and the orchids produce pollen in well-filled packets called pollinia: pollen in bulk. Pollen is expensive to make and the plant can't afford to produce the stuff on spec: the sums don't add up. The answer lies in extremely precise dispersal, and the need to find a reliable method of directed distribution has led to many complex and bizarre strategies, all designed to bring in a pollinator and then send it on to a plant of the same species as rapidly as possible. We'll look at some of these in a moment. The flowers – or the individual flowers on a spike of many – have a pronounced lip or labellum, which often operates as a landing pad for flying insects. It makes sense to spell this facility out to the potential pollinator: the labellum often carries a clear advertisement, and that explains at least some of the spectacular marks the flowers carry.

Charles Darwin – him again – was fascinated by orchids, and in 1862 published *On the Various Contrivances by which British and Foreign Orchids are Fertilised by Insects*; I've been trying for years to produce a book with a title of such length. He had a hothouse installed at his home 'Down House' in Kent. He wrote to his friend, the great botanist Joseph Hooker: 'I was never more interested in my life on any subject than this of orchids.' Darwin, it is clear, was like Mr Toad in *The Wind in the Willows,* always totally enthralled by his latest craze, but he was Toad reimagined as a genius.

So let's look at a few individual British orchids and do so with our minds on sex. What else? The word orchid is Greek for testicle; some species have an unsubtle double-swelling in the root that has given them the folk name of bollockwort, and when you see one you never pause to wonder how anyone came up with such a name. John Ruskin tried his best to clean up the study of orchids and wanted us to refer to them as 'ophrys', which means eyebrow and is the name for a genus of orchids. But it didn't catch on – and so we are left with the horrors of sex.

1. Bee orchid

This is a classic portal species: you don't get too excited about plants and then you see a bee orchid and it all changes. They're also plants that can turn a bad botanist into an orchid obsessive. They are remarkable even to human eyes because the flower looks so much like a bee. Or to be more accurate, the labellum looks like the body of a bee that is visiting the pink flower that blooms behind it. This fake bee seems to be an interesting and attractive species, with pronounced horns or antennae.

The similarity is even more remarkable if you happen to be a bee yourself, for the labellum is furry to the touch, like a real bee, and the flower also pushes out a scent remarkably similar to that of a female bee. What red-blooded male bee could resist? That is, so long as the red-blooded bee in question recognises the flower as a female of his own species: a long-horned solitary bee *Eucera longicornis*.

The real bee jumps delightedly onto the fake female and attempts to mate: technically this is pseudo-copulation. By doing so he takes on a payload of pollinia. He then moves on and if all goes well – for the plant rather than the bee – he will then try to copulate with another bee orchid. Don't be too scornful of the poor bee: human males have been known to find sexual excitement in images of human females that aren't even three-dimensional.

There's one snag. The system doesn't work without the bee, and *Eucera longicornis* is a Mediterranean species that doesn't get as far north as Britain and Ireland. But bee orchids do, and that's because they can also propagate by pollinating themselves. As Darwin pointed out, this is a suboptimal strategy and plants go to extreme lengths to avoid it. But British bee orchids have no alternative. Presumably this explains why they are prone to freakish and monstrous forms.

The bee orchid is a truly exotic plant, but it has a taste for truly unexotic locations, including roundabouts, roadside verges, spoil heaps, quarries and many different kinds of disturbed ground. They will sometimes arrive in good numbers, stay a few years and then vanish, often crowded out as a site gets overgrown, or driven out by too-eager mowing. They reached Scotland in 2003, one more example of climate change.

2. Ghost orchid

Well, one was definitely seen in 2009. Another was seen twenty-two years before that. And one might turn up again in the right spot this very summer, and then again it might not, because they can go thirty-seven years between flowerings, and maybe even longer. And don't think you can identify them from the non-flowering parts, because they haven't got any. Not above the ground, anyway. It's just that every so often, this plant, this lover of darkness and obscurity, will vary its life of underground burrowing and throw up a pale flower, apparently made from yellow wax – and nothing else.

This is the ghost orchid, a name that's not remotely fanciful. It's been considered extinct in Britain more than once, then it makes one of its occasional returns from the dead, and it takes a damned good botanist in the right place at the right time to find it. It has no chlorophyll, so it makes no attempt at photosynthesis: it has its being as an underground stem, living in darkness and throwing up a bud in the direction of the light every ten years or so, and if the weather is good the following year, this will grow into a flower-spike.

The ghost orchid, then, is a parasite. It gets all it needs from the web of mycorrhizal fungi in the soil. All orchids need fungi to germinate; many of them supplement the food they make for themselves with what they can take from fungi, but a few – including the ghost orchid – are full-time obligate parasites. The plant turns up in many places from Spain to Kamchatka and south to the Himalaya and it's rare in all of them. In Britain it turns up – when it does turn up – in deep woodland. It's been found in Herefordshire, and in Chiltern beechwoods. It's not fussy about which fungal species it parasitises, which is probably just as well. No one has ever succeeded in cultivating it.

3. Man orchid

The flowers of a bee orchid resemble a bee on purpose; the flowers of a man orchid resemble a man by pure coincidence – but it's all of a piece with the slightly sinister and faintly magical nature of the orchid family. The man orchid is one more example of orchid uncanniness: you might wonder, at least for a moment, whether you are studying botany or witchcraft; whether you are following the discipline of Charles Darwin and Joseph Hooker, or of Pomona Sprout and Severus Snape.

These plants grow 30 to 40 centimetres tall, mostly

on sunny meadows in Southeast England, and are more common on the European mainland. And they put up a spike of yellowy-green flowers, each one of which looks a little bit like a little man. They seem to have arms, legs, head and body, and hang in clusters from the stalks – a funky shape to attract pollinators.

Why, you may ask, do we call them man orchids, rather than woman orchids or little-folk orchids? The answer is obvious but seldom explained: each little man seems to possess what is, in proportion to the rest of him, an absolutely enormous penis. This is the orchid that Anthony was painting when Dan called on him: perhaps Fowles was making a subtle literary point – or maybe an unsubtle joke.

4. Lady's slipper orchid

This is a British orchid that looks the way all orchids are supposed to: damned near animals, not at all the subtle sort of thing that M liked to paint. They are crimson with a sort of yellow bladder, and they're so fabulous and lush that they were loved to the point of extinction in Britain – or near as dammit.

It was of course the custom for Victorian and Edwardian botanists to collect flowers and press them, or to dig the whole plant up. Demand rapidly outran supply and the plant was declared extinct in 1917. It turned up again in 1930 and since then, lady's slipper orchids have been guarded and protected: still there are collectors mad enough and bad enough to try and steal bits of a plant or even all of it. The bad botanist, of course, has a good heart and wouldn't dream of doing any such thing: these days most sane botanists, both good and bad, collect rare plants with a camera.

The lady's slipper orchid has been reintroduced in a dozen or so sites, most in the north of England where it grows best. The plant continues to do well across Europe and a good deal of Asia, and is classified globally as Least Concern. Though problems of habitat destruction are considerable, the real problem for the lady's slipper orchid in Britain is British lovers of lady's slipper orchids.

But you can go and see them growing wild, for there are a couple of places where access is permitted. You might have to queue and it's not exactly spontaneous, but you will get to see a spectacular plant: Kilnsey Park Estate in Yorkshire and Gait Barrows in Lancashire are good possibilities in June and July. You can find out more, of course, on the internet, and when it comes to looking for any orchid site, whether the species you are looking for is nationally rare or locally common, a few clicks will help you on your way. People are keen to put out the right sort of information these days. Your own local county wildlife trust (there's one for London too) is a very sound place to start. Make sure you join – they're all seriously good organisations.

5. Fen orchid

I have walked on water. The miracle was not in my feet but in the nature of the quaking fen beneath them: my feet sank and yet when I took another step the ground rose again. If I jumped up and down, I created waves across the land. It was like a giant waterbed, but land and water have always been fluid and interchangeable concepts in the Broads. It was here that I was shown a fen orchid, perhaps the rarest British plant I have met in person. The flowers were yellow and of a delicate complexity, looking small, wonderfully fragile and ready to go extinct at any moment.

But they haven't. They can be found at a few sites in the Broads and at Kenfig on the Welsh coast. They were declining in the Broads because of the immense difficulties of keeping a fen as a fen; given half a chance, the ecological succession will take them over, dry them out and make them unsuitable not just for fen orchids but for a suite of creatures that have evolved for this particular ecosystem. The process is hastened by water extraction for agriculture.

But great conservation work has restored a number of these wet places to their former rather sinister kind of glory. Fen orchids have been reintroduced into former sites in Norfolk and over the border in Suffolk. In a modest way, the fen orchid is making a bit of a comeback.

There is, I know, something slightly absurd about this: in order for wildflowers to bloom, we have to get involved in gardening – sometimes on a small scale, sometimes involving the whole landscape. The paradox is obvious, but it makes an equally obvious kind of sense. Since we have destroyed so many wild places, the only way to bring nature back – for its own sake and for the sake of all the humans who live in nature-deprived countries like our own – is to look after the wild places we've got and encourage more places to become wild again. We can all help: first by managing any land we might control in a kind and sympathetic way, and second, by supporting important conservation organisations like your county wildlife trust, the RSPB, Plantlife and the Woodland Trust.

Lesser celandine

DON'T BREAK THE BANK

Long live the weeds and the wilderness yet.

Gerard Manley Hopkins, 'Inversnaid'

It was 21 March, the first day of spring, and it seemed like a summons: one more walk along the Entangled Bank before I type the final full stop. It had been a dismal few weeks: cloudy, cold, lots of wind; a longish drought had been followed by copious rain. The sun was a stranger and winter clothes were still essential.

The Botanical Society of Britain and Ireland had just produced a masterpiece, modestly entitled *Plant Atlas 2020: Mapping Changes in the Distribution of the British and Irish Flora*. It told us the state of play with wild plants on these two islands, after collating more than 30 million records of 3,495 species over twenty years by 9,000 very good botanists indeed. It gave us a plain, simple, unarguable, ineluctable and irrefragable account of the way things are: what the two islands have in the way of plants and the direction in which they're heading.

The atlas shows that 53 per cent of native species of plants are in decline, and that non-native species now outnumber native species in the wild. That is not a bad thing on merely xenophobic grounds: it means that the ecosystems that support life are deeply compromised, and in many cases no longer exist. The webs of life have broken strands: they're getting weaker every day. When plants decline, the plant-eaters must do the same; those that eat the plant-eaters and those that eat the eaters of plant-eaters must also decline. The main reasons for the disaster are both simple and complex: climate change and agricultural intensification.

The changes in climate mostly affect montane plants: the plants of high places. As things warm up, the conditions that allow montane plants to thrive disappear: the evolutionary goalposts have been shifted and the plants can no longer survive. The intensification of agriculture has affected things on a much wider basis: destruction of hedges, cultivation right up to every field edge and the lavish use of insecticides, herbicides and fungicides which spread far beyond the fields into wild ecosystems, killing plants, pollinators and the dispersers of seeds.

I know, I know: we turn to nature to cheer ourselves up and then we have to face stuff like that. If nature is only going to offer more heartbreak, what's the point of it? Wouldn't it be easier to leave it alone, stay indoors, look at screens and restrict our outings to shopping malls?

There was no sun in sight as I walked the Entangled Bank. There were plenty of daffodils, mostly of the orange-trumpeted kind, a few plain yellow. A snowdrop was still in flower. The hawthorns were in leaf. May was less than six weeks off: soon we would have May blossom again and maybe even cast a clout. I noticed the arrow-shaped leaves of cuckoo pint: last year I had missed the flowers altogether, now I was recognising the plant in its vegetative state. It seemed that I'd actually learned something. And those exquisite feathery leaves – had I seen them before? I had indeed: cow parsley, not yet in flower. Nettles were springing up again: the bank was getting greener every second. The struggle for life was in full swing.

There were flowers too, flowers beyond the daffs. I found many red dead-nettles, and a single white. There were the tiny asterisks of chickweed: annual plants that will probably have set seed and vanished by the next time I looked. My eyes are getting more attuned to this botany business: I picked out a single germander speedwell, blue with a winking white eye in the centre, low to the ground. And there was a clumpy plant with many stems, again low to the ground, with starry white flowers; consultation with my phone revealed it as common whitlow grass, a member, surprisingly, of the cabbage family.

And there were lesser celandines. There were lots of lesser celandines: little golden suns all along the bank, sometimes as singletons, sometimes as constellations; one group was a small galaxy. Their message was unequivocal: no spring is dismal. I was reminded, of course, of my father, but mostly I rejoiced in spring for itself: spring and the continuation of life. These fine little plants, as common in their season as anything that lives and grows and thrives in this country, were a silent fanfare heralding the arrival of the spring.

You read important truths, like those revealed in the *Plant*

Atlas, and feel the icy hand of despair on your heart. Then you encounter an everyday miracle like a supernova of lesser celandines and you feel the exact opposite. Bloody hell, that's marvellous! We may not have as much wildness left as we would wish, but bloody hell, what we still have is worth having. What's more, it's worth saving, it's worth restoring, it's worth cherishing, it's worth looking at again and again, it's worth learning about, and it's worth all the trouble and pain and anguish of loving the bloody stuff. Bad botanists unite! If there is hope for wild nature, it's in our love for it.

ACKNOWLEDGEMENTS

Firstly, special thanks to Sara Oldfield for casting an expert eye over this book and saving me from countless howlers. I wish I too was a good botanist.

Many thanks to Ralph, who has been showing me plants and telling me their names for years. It's been a long germination, but it's borne fruit in the end.

Thanks also always to Cindy, who has drawn my eyes to plants a million times and encouraged me to write this book.

And thanks to John, tree-climbing companion on Streatham Common all those years ago.

At Simon & Schuster I owe thanks to Ian Marshall, Frances Jessop, Sophia Akhtar, Rebecca McCarthy, Clare Wallis and Loz Jerram. Special thanks for the meticulousness of Sam Stocker.

At Georgina Capel Associates thanks to Irene Baldoni and as ever to George.